Laughing

. . . And Sometimes Tears

TOBY HILLSIDE

Contents

Prologue

At a glance most would think that never a tear would escape those big brown eyes. His exterior is of a man of well built muscular composition and medium height and very strong to a fault. A voice that is always very loud and booming and to picture this man brought to tears over the past is very inspiring to hear more of what really happened in the past. I knew he had some past in his life before I married him but so did everyone. I was not prepared for the story he told me.

CHAPTER 1

Puerto Rico

1952 Puerto was on a verge of a new era

It was to have a different status in the United States of America a new law was written to make anyone who was born here a legal citizen.

Up in the quiet hills of Pueblo de Montana was a beautiful young girl ready to burst at the seams from her belly. She was so young and alone. Her husband was in the states making what little money he could to support the now growing family. He had little education and was illiterate so any work was considered precious. This young girl lived in a one room home no extra rooms at all lavatory was done outside and water was brought into the tiny home from and outside well. The only light came through a small window and candles that had been bought locally from the closest place to get any provisions.

This young girl Moya was about to give birth to her first alone, without the comfort of what most had in those days and her husband was too far away to help. Moya had found a local midwife to come and be with her. She was fortunate to find any one in the hills that had any knowledge of childbirth. Apparently the tall black Indian woman had been around the town for just this occurrence for many women in Moya's predicament. Her name was Nora. She was very tall and lean with bright eyes and a smile that would assure even the most frightened woman in this very same way. Magda said

"Stay here I am first going to get some fresh water from the spring in this here bucket. And when I get back you need to give me something you do not mind getting messy for I am surely gonna tear them up into rags to help clean and wipe you and the baby down.

Do you's have that clear missy?"

1

Moya nodded in astonishment of the prospect of finding something that she had that could be destroyed

She hardly had any possessions to start with. She looked around and decided that she could live with one sheet for the bed for now. Secretly she hopes that her demanding husband would not get upset at her choice. She knew how hard he had worked to provide her with a home of their own at such a young age. After all of the Preparations were made. Moya had a bouncing baby boy. After counting ten toes and counting ten fingers. Moya gave the little baby boy an unique name,

Diego.

The mid wife expected some sort of payment. Knowing how poor financially Moya was at the time she accepted payment of a bottle of homemade Puerto Rican rum.

CHAPTER 2

Kids cooking

Some time had gone by. Diego was at the age of boys getting into trouble and trying new things. He had made friends with one of neighborhood youngsters. His name was Poppo. He's about the same age as Diego and just a mischievous.

It was a nice spring day where the kids were home for the day, no school and Moya was off to work. Normally Diego's grandfather watched Diego and his younger brother Ishmael. But on this particular late morning, the boys were left alone to fend for themselves a bit. Gillermo Diego's grandfather saw what a nice spring day it was. Put on his favorite brown hat And lit up a hand rolled cigar and went to the closest Water, way. In Pueblo de montana there are many places where you could go fishing.

Many of the local people had to fish in order to feed their families. Crusita had gone over to the neighbor's house to gossip for a bit unknowing that, her husband had left the boys alone.

Diego was starting to get a little hungry.

"Hey, Poppo let's go inside and get something to eat."

Poppo nodded his head and went inside the little house that Diego's family lived in. The boys went into the kitchen and started to look around.

"Diego why don't you wait for your grandma to get back I know she will fix us something to eat."

Diego just shrugged his shoulders ignoring his friend and started looking for a pot to put onto the stove. After the pot was on the stove the boys searched for some food.

"You want some eggs I have some here I think I need to add some stuff so it comes out good."

Diego bent down under the Sink was bleach and some lye getting up to the stove Diego put in a few drops of bleach and decided it also needed some salt. He had seen his grandma use milk to make the eggs go further adding a little milk Diego started to mix the poisonous eggs while his young friend Poppo watched unaware that Diego had just managed to make some very potent and poisonous eggs for lunch.

A few moments went by and a neighbor by came inside after a gentle knock.

"What are you two doing? Don't you smell that awful stink?"

Diego looked at the neighbor and was surprised at the apparent stink he had made with the lunch he was getting ready to feed his friend. Luckily she had Diego open all of the windows and took the potent eggs and the pot and threw it outside.

"If you two clowns had eaten that mess you would both be found lying here on the floor dead!"

CHAPTER 3

The Circus

Some time had passed and to my happiness the Colorful circus came to town.

Or as close to our town as possible it was a three minute walk from my house to see what the ruckus was about. I grabbed my brother Ishmael and ran down the road to see what was going on.

When we got there my brother and I saw a lion in a cage. Two clowns and some Asian acrobats like nothing anyone had seen in Pablo de Montana.

The group of people entered the circus. Upon entering we saw a magicians pulling many different color handkerchiefs from his mouth.

"Wow!" I secretly thought in my mind and wondered if I could do that?

There was fire too. what a spectacle as the magician continued and pulled out of his black top hat a white pigeon. In the front, was a woman who was dressed in a ballerina costume and all the men in the town were whistling at her. She turned and wiggled her butt for all to see. She looked like a beautiful lobster with a tail. The men where all whooping and hollering at the young woman. There was a man with a loud speaker announcing an incredible feat that was going to happen. Earlier that morning some men had dug a large hole six feet down and six fit long and three feet wide.

"Now, ladies and, gentleman, we are going to put a live woman in this hole and bury her. We will cover her up good and tight so she can not get loose."

I looked at my brother who was a wide eyed as I.

The beautiful woman entered into a wooden box about the same size as a coffin. After she got in and closed the lid to the wooden box. The men lowered the beautiful young woman into the hole dug earlier that day.

"Tomorrow come and see what happens when we dig her up. See the incredible trick you will whiteness it here for the first time ever!" shouted the ringmaster to the crowd.

The next day early. My brother and I hurriedly did our chores and dressed. We did not want to miss the next trick. We ran to the place where the amazing feat was about to be unfolded right before our very eyes, such excitement I could barely control myself. It was frightening and interesting at the same time I believe my brother was just as afraid as I was.

The crowd gathered and waited for the ring master to show. The magician came up the way smiling just as confident as ever. The acrobats were twirling and some of them were blowing billows of fire. Wow it was amazing. The magician came up to center stage and asked.

"Can I have two volunteers?" Looking around the group two men raised their hands.

Fautino one of my fathers friends and Victor my uncle raised his hand as well. They were both handed shovels to start to undo the ground where the beautiful young woman had been buried alive the day before.

I really thought that no one could stand that much time under the ground with out surely dying. I was worried that they would actually dig up a dead woman and not one alive. I looked over at my brother to see if he looked as worried as I was. The digging began and we all watched in horror as the time seemed to slip away after what appeared to be a life time but in reality was only a half hour the box was dug up.

The two men stepped back a bit and the Magician came to the box and the two helpers lifted the box out of the ground and laid it by the side of the hole. Leaning over the top the magician lifted the lid. Silence was everywhere with anticipation.

"I bet she is dead." Said one of the spectators another further back also exclaimed

"I bet she did not live through this."

While the group was murmuring the magician leaned over the box put out his hand and the lady inside grabbed his hand and gentle came out slowly. She was alive!!! But also naked!!! The magician turned her around very quickly and she was in the red bikini that they had buried her into earlier the day before. Applauding was heard very loud while the lady in the box danced around to prove to everyone that she was okay.

After the circus had left and the town had a chance to reflect on the activities. My brother and I left to play on our own. It would turn out to be, rather interesting to say the least.

My younger brother and I got a long wonderfully and as always played together making up games or imitating things like small children did.

We tied a rope to one end to one house and the other end to the other end believing we could tight rope walk like the acrobats did at the circus.

That did not work so instead we needed a longer rope. We let the two family cows loose by untying their rope. After, we tied one end of the rope to a tree in the back yard. And the other end of the rope to another tree. The cows were free all of this time. I am sure the cows were wondering what happens now.

Our parents were not working so getting things from the house were easy we went inside we took my mother's mattress off of her bed since it was bigger than mine. Afterwards we pulled the mattress out, of the house.

We put it under the rope where we had tied from tree to tree. I climbed the tree branches up pretty high and made my way to the rope that was secured with the mattress waiting for me below in case I fell. I crossed the rope without falling and made it to the other side.

"Wow Diego you could work in the circus that is great. It is my turn let me try."

My younger brother climbed the tree and was looking down at the tight rope we had fastened to the trees."

Don't be afraid!" "Don't be afraid!"

Just as I said that my brother fell onto the mattress bruising his shoulder.

"Hey are you all right?"

Getting up from the mattress we decided to take my mothers mattress back to her bed. Neither, of us, taking the time needed to clean the mattress off. I climbed up and retrieved the rope we borrowed from the cows.

I re- roped the cows that managed to not move and stayed corralled.

"Diego what was your favorite part of the circus?"

"I liked the part when they buried that woman. I have an idea. Here is a great plan let's go and find a shovel you can bury me. And look for me the next day just like the circus."

Ishmael looked at me smiling at my great idea.

"Ask grandpa and grandma if they have one but don't say what you want it for. Okay"

We looked in the barn and around the yard and even near the horses.

"Grandpa Do you have a shovel?" I asked.

"No Diego I leave my shovel at the factory."

My brother and I tired looking for the shovel that was to burry me that day. Their, was no shovel found and I was not buried.

CHAPTER 4

The Green Kite

Some time had passed since the summer I was still a youngster enjoying my youth. I remember the green kite in particular only because after flying it one day everything for me changed as innocence would change anyone.

In the back yard I was clad in nothing but my jeans barefoot barechested. Enjoying the green kite I had made out of the top of an old shoe box and colored it green with the most recent purchase of crayola's fastened a thread to it to hang on when it was up in flight and used some worn out old sheet and cut into strips to make a tail. For a handmade kite it flew quite well.

Watching my homemade kite up in the air and just enjoying being a boy with no worries my mother stuck her head out the back door and said Cocoa was calling for me.

"Maybe she wants me to run to the store." I thought as I charged over there. As I arrived to Cocoa's home she waved for me to enter. She was alone with no children or husband and lived right next door and would at times ask either me or my brother to fetch her things from the store. This would give us some pocket change at times for doing the errand. On this day things were a little different Cocoa waved me into her home and I entered. She was not wearing anything but a see-through nightgown I wondered if she realized that I could see her silhouette underneath the thin garment.

"Diego come back here I want to show you something." Cocoa walked towards her bedroom.

As I entered her room she whipped off her nightgown with a flourish. I stood there frozen in the spot on the floor not knowing what to think.

She glanced over at me and removed my trousers, picked me up like a rag doll and fell with me onto her bed both of us naked. I was not sure what to think or what to do it frightened me I subjected my self to her groping. She groped my body entering her tongue into all of the crevasses my nose, eyes, mouth. As swift as a ninja she quickly grabbed my head and put it between her legs to see her vagina with her juices flowing and the curly hairs. Looking at this site excited me and my cock got hard. I was fearful that Cocoa was seeing this. She was hoping that this would happen.

She grabbed me up like a rag doll and thrusted my hardened member into her waiting opening thrusting ever so hard and not letting go. I was in so much pain during all of this and embarrassed. Letting me up finally and handing me my pants. Cocoa did not say anything more except.

"Do not tell anyone about this."

I left her house scarred emotionally and in pain. I headed to my home.

Usually my mother would fix hot chocolate at night for me and my brother for a treat and I could smell the chocolate when I entered the house.

"Diego I made you chocolate. Do you want some?"

I entered quickly to my room and said.

"No I do not want any chocolate."

Mom went into the living room to watch TV. I examined my self after being abused and tortured. I saw to my horror that I was bleeding from my penis, still in pain I stripped off my pants and threw them under the bed. Hopping onto the bed and still scared and scarred I pulled the sheet up over my head. The next morning I did not go to, school but choose to hide the evidence of what occurred the evening before. The sheet to my bed was covered in blood like my jeans. I found a hoe in the garden and went to the back yard and buried the evidence close to the outhouse. Never to be found or mentioned ever again.

CHAPTER 5

(Juan Baptista Day)

It was June 24th and I was about twelve interested in the things all young boys are. I decided to go to the beach Porto Nuevo or in English New Port beach. It would be a great time to go since this was the evening that all Islanders in Puerto Rico celebrated, Juan Baptista day. I knew that there would be a lot of activity which there always was on this special day. For those of you who don't know who Juan the Baptist was.

He was the patron saint that baptized Jesus Christ. They called him John the Baptist. I left my house around six in the evening because of it being in the summer we still had a great amount of daylight left so walking to the beach was easy.

As I arrived at the beach I noticed that there were so many people there young and old. People with large quantities of food I could tell by the wonderful aroma of roasting pigs. Some women would bring rice and beans or sweet rice with mike and cinnamon one of my personal favorites some people had little fires lit so they could see when night falls. This celebration could last over night and into the next morning. There were taverns close by too if you wanted to bring beer or any other type of alcoholic beverages to the beach you could. There were some crazy people too I think because I could have sworn I heard gunshots in the air.

I thought to myself that it had to be one of the old timers from my town they never seemed to have any idea how crazy some of the shit they did.

As I was taking in the sights and breathing in all the different smells I managed to almost bump into a few of my friends from my neighborhood. They were Manos Rapido, Tato, And Carpio

"He guys I am glad I caught you here. What are you doing?"

11

Manos Rapido exclaimed

"We are here checking out the beach and all the people. There has to be at least a thousand people here. Did you see all the cars?"

"Yes it is great right?" I asked my friend.

He nodded and smiled a giant smile showing all of his teeth and Said "Hey guys, I have a plan. Want to know what it is?"

Naturally being curious I asked

"What?"

"Look around see all the women in the water

Swimming? If we go into the water where it is dark we could probably touch on their privates. They would think it was fish touching them."

"What do you mean exactly?" I asked my friend and cocking my head to the side. I thought I knew what he meant but I wanted to be sure.

"Well there is hardly any light and lots of ladies in the water in bathing suits think of it man. We could jump in the water and sneakily grab them between their legs they would never know it was us and at the same time we can see what a real woman feels like there."

Running down to the beach edge where the four of us decided we were going to go along and do this we all got into the water and swam around. I noticed that Manos Rapido had already started touching some women because a few had jumped almost out of the water. Since I wanted to not appear as a coward to my buddies I dove into the water and found the first woman. I decided to play it safe and touch her on her thigh first. I figured if I did not get slammed I would go to the next woman and aim for something different. Since the first woman only jumped a little and did not hit me I made my way to the next lady. I swam as quietly as I could with out making any noise and reached up and grabbed her right between her legs and quickly swam away. I had courage now and decided to touch a couple more women between their legs. "Oh what fun." I thought in my head that maybe I would get caught and someone would surly tell there husband or boyfriend and getting a brutal beating.

I went on the beaches edge as I watched the different woman jump and scream I heard one woman say

"Oh my goodness it is boys touching us."

The other woman exclaimed

"Oh it is only babies playing."

After a good while I just knew that there would be some trouble and I could see in the distance a lady punching the water and jumping up and down and screaming something I am not sure just what. Shortly after, I saw the lady slapping hard at the water and kicking. Manos Rapido came out of the water now sporting a black eye and scratches on his face. The rest of the gang followed.

"Hey we better get out of here before some boyfriends beat us up if any of those women tell them they were touched in their privates."

"I am ready to go too man let's get out of here." looking forward to not being caught anymore we all left and managed to arrive at our homes unscathed.

CHAPTER 6

Family

After school Ishmael and I would go to our grandparent's home and stay there until my mother returned from working at the china factory. My brother and I would sit on the living room floor and enjoy watching some of our favorite cartoons.

While we did that our grandfather would sit on the front porch enjoying one of his fresh hand rolled cigars. Usually our grandmother would bring us the most delicious hand made guava cookies or cheese.

My grandmother was a beautiful woman that stood about 5'3" with long jet black hair to her shoulders. She was a native Taino Indian of Puerto Rico She had given birth to thirteen children some did not make it I am not sure how many may not have made it all the way to child birth.

She and my grandfather were both very religious and went to Mass every Sunday. Quiet, and, very loving. My grandfather was around 5'9 his skin was more of a chocolate color grandmas coloring was much lighter. He always used his favorite brown hat and was always, happy. Sometimes my brother and I would enjoy sitting on grandpa's lap from time to time.

I remember asking him

"Grandpa did the money tree leave you any money today?"

"I have to check in the back yard Diego to see I don't think so. Let me go look." He would saunter back there and shaking his head no when he returned "Sorry boys no money today ask me in a few weeks I think the money tree may need a little more time to grow."

Satisfied, with that we would wait the two weeks and then enquire about the money tree again. Grandpa would then put his hands in his pockets and come out with two shinny dimes for me and my brother. We would race each other to the corner store where an abundance of candies was sold. Sometimes we would get coconut candy or pineapple candy two of my favorite flavors. Once in a while my grandparents would take a journey on the public car into town these trips would cost five cents each way five cents there and back. They would bring back with them Pineapples, Bananas, and Apples. Apples don't grow in Puerto Rico so that was always a special treat for us. Most of the time, they would eat what they grew on their eight acre farm. They even had some goats, pigs, and cows, not sure what other animals were there. They would make rice and beans and fish what was really great was grandma would fry the fish in coconut oil yum yum! For beverages we would use the empty cans that contained beans mostly and would wash them out good and make sure that there were no rough edges. Usually the choice of beverage was water, coffee, or Kool-Aid.

My grandmothers house had an old pot belly stove where she cooked by putting dry kindling wood into the belly.

Grandpa would first toast these beans Idionda beans until they were dry and later would ground them into powder this coffee had a wonderful cherry flavor. When ever we drank coffee it was always enjoyed black. Sometimes my grandfather or grandmother would grind the corn they had into flour that would last for months.

This particular grinding device my grandfather made by hand using two very large stones what a site not too many people today use this method anymore just the old timers. The trees on the land were Guava, Mango, Tamarindo, Papaya, Guananbana, Acerda, and passion fruit trees a great selection especially if you love fruit.

After mom would return from work she would spend a short while talking with my grandparents. we would leave my grandparents home and head to our house my thoughts always went to the fact that grandma and grandpa's house and home was like heaven I hated leaving and going to our own home because their was a devil living there. Who was he?

My father had an odd look to him a very tiny head with real small ears like you would see on some of the dinosaurs like a T-rex or a brontosaurus. He had long gangly arms and legs like a giant octopus what my mother saw in him? I still d not know.

My father treated us I like we were prisoners and in a slave camp with a crazy person running the show. Dad worked in the local Sugar cane field and never seemed to sit he even ate dinner standing up. He was never tired and always looking to drink rum or beer.

Getting home my father was in his dusty, dirty, clothes and, dusty dirty boots. He was about 6'3" a tall man I should say. I do not think I ever saw my father smile. Many times he would beat my mother I remember when she was pregnant with my younger brother he kicked her right in the stomach I sometimes wonder if there was even a reason he did any of his craziness'. I believe out of divine intervention my brother was born without any problems. It was a current theme of the week my dad would grab the branch from the Pendula tree. These trees have thick branches and are very hard. I would get beaten by the branches off that tree everyday. I was still a growing teenager and I guess either he had more than enough, to drink and with his steel toed boots kicked me right in my testicles as hard as he could. This was without any provocation he just did this with out warning and with out notice. The pain was so severe I dropped to the floor unconscious. What a horrible pain that left me in my groin area for what seemed like a very long time. I remember one time or more than once I was in my bed not bothering anyone and I saw my father towering over me at the foot of my bed with a rubber hose in his hand and with out any hesitation he swung that dam hose over and over and beat me to a pulp I felt my skin rip under the blows when he was done with my back he would flip me over and keep on beating me until I had welts all over my body front and back.

I asked "Why are you doing this?"

I think because I was questioning him he grew more agitated and hit me more so. While he continued to beat me on my back this way he had his cigar in his mouth and you could smell the booze coming from the pores of his skin, it smelled like cheap rum this night. The following day after this assault there was more to come some nights more severe then others. After the happy time at my grandparents he came at me with his leather belt using it where the buckle end was to hit me he swung that buckle belt at my head and everywhere else I just could not escape his blows.

I remember trying to endure this with out yelling or crying for fear the blows would get worse. You would think I would mention this to my grandparents because it would happen everyday in those years you minded your parents no matter how crazy they were this went on for years. I should have said something maybe my life would have turned out different who knew. I believe my mother was very much afraid of him otherwise if she was stronger she would have prevented this abuse of assaults to continue. I believe this because she never mentioned one word of this to her parents or anyone else.

One Saturday morning in April my mother, and brother had to go into town and see the dentist. I was left alone with my father.

On this day the sky was blue just like the ocean and the clouds looked like little puffy kittens. I looked through the kitchen window through the divider I could see my snoring, sleeping, drunk father on the bed. I thought to myself.

"While this bastard is asleep I have the time to kill him. I just need to make sure he is good and asleep."

I went into the house and into the kitchen the only thing I could think to use to murder my father was the lone kitchen knife it was the only type of weapon that would do the job. I took the knife in my right hand and started to walk to the bedroom where my father was sleeping.

At the exact same time a horrific noise was overhead it was shaking the whole entire house I ran outside still with the knife in my hand. Looking up to the sky to my amazement flying very low to the ground was a 747 Pan Am jumbo jet oh what a sight. I went back into the house and I started to think differently. I don't know if that was me or the voice that I heard say.

"Get out of here and forgive your father!" was that the voice I heard or had the airplane been a message to me?

I realized at that exact moment I needed to leave.

Leaving the house I ran into Bautista Soler just a neighborhood person I knew and he told me that they were looking for some people to work on the farms in Delaware cutting and tending the Asparagus plant on the farm there.

"How can I do that I don't have the money for the ticket?" I said almost defeated to my neighbor friend.

"Try asking Dino the grocery store owner I am sure he will lend it to you Diego it is only 45 dollars."

"Okay I will talk to him and I will let you know if I get the loan for forty five dollars."

I knew in my mind if I got it or not I was never going back.

CHAPTER 7

Tuesday

April 29, 1969

I went to see Dino for the loan I needed to get on
The Pam Am flight. Dino owned the local grocery store in town. He
was a kind man with a friendly face built like a healthy man of his age. I
went in to the store.

"What happened Diego" Dino asked. Maybe by the look on my face
he knew something was wrong. I swallowed hard and asked.

"Can I borrow forty five dollars from you? I need it to get the plane
that is taking people to work on the farms in Delaware. The airfare is
forty five dollars I just don't know where I will find that kind of money."

"Diego I can loan it to you but do you think you would be able to
pay me back? I would want sixty dollars in return."

"Sure no problem, I will send it to you as soon as I get paid."

Dino must have sensed something was wrong but maybe he just
could not put his finger on it.

"Give me thirty one time and then thirty the next."

"No, you have been so good to lend me this money I will be happy to
send you the full sixty at once."

Dino handed me two twenty dollar bills and a five and took the
paper money and folded it very tight and put it safely in my jean pocket. I
left the little grocery store happy knowing I had now the money I needed
to pay for the trip. I glanced up at the sky and there in the billows of
some very fluffy clouds I could make out a figure of an angel in the sky. I
kept on walking until I was at my friend Bautista's house. He was sitting
outside on the front porch to the house.

"Hey man I found the money Coo lent it to me."

Coo was the nickname we all had for the local shop owner.

"I knew he would lend it to you I already put your name on the list."

The next day Bautista came to my house.

"Everything is ready we have to be at the airport by 8:30 so we should probably take the public car to get there in time. The flight is scheduled to take off at 9:15 am in the Pan Am jumbo 747 jet."

My friend left. I was there with conflicting emotions not too sure of what I just did the unknowing was starting to scare me some. That night I told my mother what I intended to do going to the kitchen where mom usually was I told her.

"I am going to leave tomorrow to work in Delaware the farmer their needs help with his Asparagus crop."

Waiting for some kind words of expression but not really getting any my mother looked up at me and asked

"What about school Diego your not going to finish school?" She asked.

I wasn't sure how to respond but I knew what had to be done. Truthfully I did not want to leave behind my mother, brother and especially my grandparents. The last words that evening my mother said to me was.

"If that is what you want to do."

God knew what I had to do I needed to get away before something horrible was to happen. That was the reason for my decision to leave. The night before I could not sleep I tossed and turned and thought about what tomorrow would be like. I thought about how young I was and the simple fact that I only knew three or four words of English. I knew words like pencil, desk, and teacher would not really help me in the real world. The morning came quickly the rooster was crowing out side to let us all know it was five am in the morning. I jumped out of bed excited and nervous at the same time. I washed my face, brushed my teeth and hair.

I put on the only pair of jeans I owned with two patches on the left knee the other on the back right below my butt cheek. This was really the only pair of pants I owned in the world I put on my blue t-shirt same as pants the only one I had I did not have a suitcase but I did find a shopping bag and put in a towel and grabbed my toothbrush and the families soap.

This would leave them with nothing since that was all we had and I grabbed the only small tube of toothpaste the family had. What choice did I have really?

Put on my shoes. Well if you could call them shoes these were keds and they were already grungy and really needed to find the nearest garbage can. But they were all that I had so I went with them on my feet.

My mother left for work followed by the octopus to the sugar cane field and my brother left for school. The only one in my family for the moment that knew I was leaving was my mother. I hated not telling my brother what I was doing but I needed this to be my idea and I did not want to tangle with the octopus or the devil about the prospect of his personal punching bag leaving town. I walked outside after everyone left and headed up the road. I could see my grandparent's front door was opened and I wanted to tell them both I was leaving. I went inside and my grandfather was drinking coffee from the bean can sitting at the table. My grandmother was ironing clothes with a hot iron.

"Grandpa I am leaving in a few minutes to work on a farm in Delaware."

My grandfather handed me a cup of hot black coffee like his and sat me down with him in the kitchen and gave me some good wisdom. I could see that he was worried by the expression on his face and tears trying not to escape his eyes.

"Diego before you go let me give some grandfatherly advice behave and never be a bother always be polite and do the best you can. I want you to have a happy long life. I hope everything turns out good for you my boy. Go with God and remember that I and your grandmother love you very much."

They both came to my side as I stood up to leave and hugged me in unison. A few minutes later outside the public car arrived and my friends and I left for the airport. As we rode I was very depressed and sad not sure of what was going to unfold as the day progressed. I felt my right ear get a little warm and a voice I had heard before

Said "Do not be afraid my son everything will be all right."

After hearing this voice I felt a little calmer. Around 8:30 am they started to load the air plane my friends and I got in line and we were the last few that entered the airplane.

I was shocked at the grand size the plane was inside there were about five hundred passengers that day. It was mostly men with work clothes and ready to go working on the fields in a place I had never been. I had never seen so many people at one time with the same idea in mind to work on a farm. I noticed that I was not the only passenger with a shopping bag. There were young stewardesses on the plane helping everyone into their seats. She helped me and my friends too at the same time I sat down my heart started to beat fast and for a moment I thought about running right back out of the airplane. My ear got warm again and the voices returned.

"Do not be afraid my son all will be well." I could feel the plane starting to roll slowly down the runway.

The microphone over head had a voice coming from it.

"Good morning everyone this is your captain today. Please fasten your seatbelt s and return to your seats we will be taking off in a few minutes to Newark New Jersey we should arrive in approximately 2 hours the temperature in Newark this morning is a crisp forty five degrees please enjoy the flight." The voice left the air.

As the plane reached the runway I noticed that everyone got pretty quite. A huge noise came from the belly of the plane and take off. We were flying high in the air I looked out the window to see the ground and right before my very eyes the ground disappeared. I started to sweat and my hands got clammy.

Another announcement

"We are going to fly at 43,000 feet"

Another jolt, to my heart, that was beating very fast. I felt my body get cold and I knew it was strictly from the fear I had about the prospect of flying for the first time. This was so much more grater than when my brother and I would swing from tree top to tree top for goodness sake we were 43,000 feet in the air yikes! As the plane was in the 43,000 feet the stewardess announced on the microphone

"Gentlemen you may now unbuckle your seatbelts and move freely around the cabin."

The travelers in the plane all started to relax and talked loudly joking and lighting up cigarettes. Some had rum and other sorts of booze in their paper bags and started to drink as well. I just sat there quietly and prayed for my family and for myself and what was ahead. I felt my ear warm up again and the voices returned.

"You did the right thing. This is the same airplane that flew over your house when you were about to kill you father."

About an hour had passed and the stewardess came to everyone with sandwiches and soda or rum or other forms of alcohol I was given a tuna fish sandwich with lettuce and tomatoes and also was handed a 7-up.The other travelers on the flight were now buying rum and what ever else was available with alcohol in it.

The other travelers were getting louder, and, drunker and, laughing loudly now. I sat reflecting about the abuse I escaped and not sure what type of life I was about to find in the very near future.

"Buckle your seats belts please we are about to land in approximately ten minutes the temperature is a brisk forty five degrees."

I just happened to glance out the window and saw what looked like dense fog I started to get nervous not knowing how it was possible the pilot could see through all of the fog let alone land an airplane safely. I was scared to death! Finally what seemed like a lifetime to me but was only ten minutes or so I could feel the wheels of the airplane hit the runway and we taxied to the gate. We were parked at gate number 8. Another announcement

"Thank you for flying Pan Am"

I got up out of my seat and walking into the sleeve of the gate I could feel the cool weather deep in my bones since I only had on thread bare clothes. Luckily inside the airport it was warm. Inside the airport was like another world so many people so much commotion there were farmers apparently waiting for this particular aircraft that had all the workers on it. Each farmer had a sign with which they were what farm and a list of names. My farmer or soon to be boss was Mr. Green he introduced himself in Spanish to my relief. I was still a little afraid but at the same time happy that I would be able to understand him and he would be able to understand me. He was a pretty tall thin man wearing kaki green clothing and had on his a head a blue baseball cap. I noticed he was sporting a big cigar in his mouth and most of the other farmers seemed to like the pipe instead. After he called the names of my friends and I he explained he had forty other workers on the farm already some of them were black men and some were Spanish men maybe form other parts of the world at this time I just did not know.

"Let's go get your suitcases." Farmer Green said.

We all just shrugged our shoulders and held up the shopping bags we all seemed to have instead of the typical suitcase. Farmer Green had a hardy laugh and said

"Okay so I see you are ready for work then!"

CHAPTER 8

Mashed potatoes and Turkey

We left the airport my friends, Bautista, Chachi, Manuel, Candido and me. And followed Mr. Green out to the parking lot where there was a short bus waiting. We rode what seemed to be a long time but in reality it was three and a half hours. Mr. Green was driving the bus and pulled over to the side of the road.

"Boys we are going to stop here and get something to eat. Why don't you take a moment to stretch your legs and maybe use the men's room if you have to?"

Mr. Green said to us as he jumped off the bus stretching his own tired legs. My friends and I entered into the restaurant on the side of the road. Inside was a beautiful youngish woman her blonde hair tied up in a bun. I just happened to notice how sparkling blue her eyes were. She had on a brown uniform with a white apron and low heeled brown shoes. The type of shoe a person would wear not to slip on a wet or greasy floor.

Mr. Green greeted the waitress by her first name Cindy.

"Hello Cindy I have some fine young fellows that are pretty hungry, don't worry about the bill the tab will all be on me."

Now turning around to me and my friends Mr. Green spoke to us in our native tongue and explained. "Order what ever you want. Don't worry about the bill I will pay for it. Eat; I will be just outside here making a few phone calls." Mr. Green said to us focusing now on the telephone that was outside against the wall to the restaurant. "As soon as I am done I will come back inside."

Now leaving my friends and I me alone in a restaurant. Cindy motioned to us with her hand to follow her. We obliged and followed into the dinning room where there were different types and sizes of tables all

25

ready laid out with table cloths and silver ware. She showed us a table that would accommodate us because it had five chairs, along with five place settings. After she sat us all down she put five Menus on the table. My friends and I never being in a restaurant of any kind until now were all at a loss as what were the right things you do in a place such as this.

After we received the menus Cindy waited with her hand folded across her chest looking at my friends and to me and moving her head from left to right. My friends and I keep looking at the menu for what appeared to be a very long time. Cindy our waitress left us and she went into possibly the kitchen where they prepared food. Perhaps she thought we were a bunch of retards and had to ask her boss or manager how to handle us. Not one of us understood a word of English nor read it on the menu we all had. Cindy came over to me first and laid the Menu down in front of me showing me to point with my pointer finger and the selections to order. Since I did not know any English I pointed to something on the menu hoping that it would be agreeable. Candito, Manuel, and Chachi all followed and ordered the same as I with their pointer fingers.

Bautista asked me

"Diego can you put your finger on the menu for me? I could eat just about anything."

I decided to pass my finger at the same place I had just ordered my entrée. Cindy took our finger orders after some time and left us alone.

One of my friends asked me

"Diego what did you order?"

I answered "How stupid are you? I have no idea." I quietly thought to myself that my friends were starting to resemble the comics on TV the Three Stooges.

Now Candito asked Chachi the same question

Chachi answered

"I don't know either."

Candidto "Me either."

"I eat anything!" My friend Bautista said with a grin.

"Hey man don't say that what if she brings you boiled dick or something?" Candito snickered.

My two friends Bautista, and Candito where on their feet, ready to have a tussle. Manuel and I grabbed our friends and sat them back in their chairs.

"Hey don't fight here. I know you two can not swim all the way back to Puerto Rico if there is trouble." I said with authority trying to get my friends to settle down. We will know what we ordered when the food gets here."

No sooner did I say that when Cindy walked back with hot food on her serving tray for all. Not one of us knew English, in any form the surprise and suspense was about to end. Placed down in front of me was a beautiful plate of food. Items of food I had never eaten in my life but it was sooooo! Good I had managed to finger order a plate of mashed potatoes; turkey slices with gravy some vegetables and a red thing that you call cranberry sauce. One of my, favorite meals ever since. Bautista was just as happy as I with what I had ordered him. Consequently the other three friends had all ended up with spaghetti and meatballs not bad for finger ordering. We finished our meals and Cindy cleared away the dishes and returned shortly after with what was a smaller menu with pictures of the dessert this was easier for us it had different fruits on it. I like apples I finger ordered what I thought would be just an apple. To my delight it was an apple pie first one I ever had boy was that great. After we were finishing up dessert Mr. Green came over to our table.

"Did you boys get enough to eat?"

My friends and I thanked him for our meals. I had to speak now because I had this thought on my mind.

"You know Mr. Green it is a good thing we all have fingers."

Mr. Green now had a funny look on his face and stared at what I had just uttered. I continued to speak up

"Otherwise we would have had a problem because we had to order from the menu with our fingers. Cindy showed us that way because we had no other choice not knowing the language here."

Mr. Green now took his cigar out of his mouth and burst into very loud laughter.

"Boys I am so sorry I forgot you don't know English, with that Mr. Green turned red like a tomato.

Mr. Green now cleared his throat

"You know your right because if you get a speck of dust in your eye you need your finger to get it out. If I went to Puerto Rico I would be okay because I know the language there. But if I had to go somewhere like China I guess boys I would have to order with my finger too and hope for the best."

CHAPTER 9

The Asparagus Farm

The way to the campground, my, friends and, I were about, to start working. They fell asleep. I think I was too wired or maybe it was a little bit of fear on my part not knowing what was in store for me for the next few months. Mr. Green and I started a conversation to pass the time.

"You know Diego my wife Nancy and I love Puerto Rico. They have some wonderful food. Oh man and the way you Puerto Rican's cook wonderful. I see that the island has ideal soil too. I noticed too that a lot of the fruit is grown natural without a lot of chemical treatment I wonder if your island brother's realize what a wonderful Island Puerto Rico is?"

We chatted a little more about different fruit trees and plants and different parts of Puerto Rico and the places Mr. Green and his wife Nancy had been to. It felt good just to relax and talk for a little while on the little bus.

We made it to the camp ground where we were to stay for the spring and summer and there were it seemed to me about thirty or so men. They were of different color or, nationality. We were all shown the beds we sere to sleep in these were stacked bunk beds that lined the walls.

Mr. Green asked me

"Diego do you want the top or the bottom bunk?"

I answered him quickly and said "the top bunk."

"I don't blame you Diego now your talking I always like to be on top too. "As he chuckled, under his breath.

The first night there it was pretty cold getting comfortable was impossible. I only had my thread bare clothing and never thought I would have to bring a winter blanket to get through a cold night like this one. What did I know about these cold night's here in this strange land?

The bunk house did not have any heat, no one had a car to run into town to get blankets or something more appropriate to sleep comfortably in nor was there any extra money at this time to even purchase such items.

The next morning started real early we all were up what appeared to be before any rooster. It was still dark. We crossed the camp to another large building where there was food for all of us to eat. Oatmeal, coffee and some rolls. After eating breakfast we all loaded into a small bus that would take us to the field. This was an old school bus that held the whole bunch of us. The ride took about twenty minutes give or take. The driver's name was Felix. He was heavy set man with dark skin smoking a pipe wearing dark sunglasses and sporting an orange baseball cap. I don't think it was for any team that played baseball. Maybe he just liked that color. We got off the bus and Felix walked with us into the field to show us how to cut the asparagus plant correctly. Felix had a strange knife that looked like a spatula fork just very sharp and it was used to cut the Asparagus plant all the way at the bottom.

"Okay gentlemen what you have to do is just follow the lines that you see to the end where there is a box to fill. Don't worry about looking back. Once you cut one go to the next and keep on going until you get to the end."

I bent down and got started with the task at hand and maybe it was curiosity or ignorance I don't know which but I looked back. Don't you know all the places I had already cut were Asparagus plants standing up as if to say

"FUCK YOU!"

Boy what a strange plant this is. It appeared the plants all of them were giving me the middle finger! As the boxes at the end of the rows were filled there were others that put the boxes onto a tractor that brought the asparagus back to the packing house. Felix sat in the old school bus reading the paper when we finished one field he would bring us to the next one. As I worked on the bending and cutting I could not help but realize just how much I did not like what I was going to do for the rest of the season I grasped at my will and prayed to God every time I took a very short break I would look to the heavens and pray

"Help me God with this heavy load I know with you all things are possible."

And I would continue to do the job I had before me. But I prayed that same prayer many times and after a month or so had passed the work became easier for me to manage.

My friend Bautista always complained about his back hurting. Chachi complained about his back too. Chachi was the tallest and the thinnest of all of us and I could understand for him that bending all day would be a problem, while he worked he had his mouth open.

When Chachi talked he had his mouth open. Even when he was standing there like a big dummy he had his mouth open. He reminded me of a big fish in the pond back home. Candido, the oldest one of us he never complained he was fifty years old and short in stature but had a big melon head. Candido always managed to be six or seven men ahead of us. I managed to get as good as Candido and one day Candido said to me

"Diego look at these young kids and probably stronger. They are all complaining like old ladies."

My friend Manuel called Candido the little champ.

Manuel drank more water than all of us. He wore a big white cowboy hat in the field and I wondered if that helped him to stay cool. That quickly changed when I saw in reality how much water he drank. I continued working and bending and once in a while I would reflect on my life I left behind in Puerto Rico. Once a week when we all had a day off we would take the three hour walk into town to buy things like cigarettes, beer, and some toiletries. Some of us would call home Candido since he was the oldest and drinking age would buy for me at times Budweiser beer. After our purchases we would walk back drinking the beer on the way.

Daily when the work was done some of us would shower in the stalls only cold water was provided I made sure I showered when ever I got the chance.

Others for some reason did not shower I wonder if they had any ideas how bad they smelled I don't think it bothered any of them. The ones that did not shower I mean being younger than most I kept quiet about this.

Saturday evening was pay day. My first week I made 97.00 dollars which was back then 1.40 an hour minus the money subtracted for the three meals and the cot to sleep on. The first thing I bought was the 60 dollar money order and sent it to Coo the local merchant in my town that had lent me the money to escape.

One Monday while I was in the field working late in the afternoon a large passenger jumbo jet passed over head. I dropped my knife I was working with and was immediately transformed to seeing myself back in Puerto Rico standing in my mother's house with knife in my hand ready to kill my sleeping father. Candido noticed that the look on my face had changed when this all occurred while the plane passed overhead. Candido spoke up.

"Diego you okay man you just turned two or three shads of grey." I ignored his question and tried to gather myself. I took a breath and just shook my head that I was all right. When a plane flies overhead I still think of that day. When, the large plane stopped me; from doing, the, unimaginable. I thought quietly to myself in that field where I could have ended up instead if I had acted on the thoughts I had that day. After I got back to work I felt a nice warm breeze and a young voice that sounded like an angel said to me

"Diego you are going to be okay do not be afraid my son. I will always be with you."

After the voice passed I had a thought that came over me. I remembered that my uncle Victor lived in Littletown New York and I happened to have his phone number. I decided I would call him next Saturday and see if I could avoid at all cost going back to Puerto Rico when the Asparagus farm work was done. Saturday arrived and I made the three hour walk to the phone and called.

"Hello Victor this is Diego I am here in the united states working in Delaware on an Asparagus farm. The work will be done in a week or so and I was wondering if you had any ideas. Maybe work or something so I do not have o go back to Puerto Rico."

Silence for a moment and then my uncle answered me

"Diego I have an idea when you get here you can spend a night or two and then I know a big giant farm in Orange Island New York that is always looking for workers. I can take you there and introduce you to the owners and then we can see what they say. It isn't far from Littletown but you will see when you get here. Call me when you get into town. I will pick you up at the bus stop and we will take it from there. Is that okay with you?"

I was very happy to hear this and agreed.

"Yes I will call you one week before and when I get there thank you. You know I like work I am not afraid of it. I will see you in a couple of weeks."

"Okay Diego I am looking forward to it seeing you soon."

Hanging up the phone I knew I had another mystery to work out in my life but I was not going back home I felt very reserved but also happy that I had some sort of plan to follow in the next few weeks ahead,.

CHAPTER 10

Pincone Island

Orange Island is farm land in upstate New York not too many people know about it unless you have been there. Every year immigrant farm workers go there to work the fields of black dirt usually the onions you find at any local big super market and lettuce. The area has been known to be called the black dirt farms it's because the dirt is black in color and rich like a good cup of coffee. Close to the onion farms was also a dairy farm called Angels on Polanski highway.

I left the Asparagus farm in Delaware and found my uncle Victor in Littletown with out any problem. I was glad to be looking forward to something new and a little nervous. But looking back I realized that I showed my self that I had great reserve to do almost anything. Victor and I arrived to Orange Island farm land it looked very subtle and quiet

My uncle and I went to one of the offices of the owner of Grass farm Ramon a very reserved and quiet man of a stocky build heavy but muscular his brother was the second in command the other brother Jimmy tall and thin and seemed to walk rather swiftly when out on the field or the street or anywhere for that matter. Ramon agreed that I could stay and work there.

"Diego let me show you around. I have to tell you that a lot of the workers have gone home to their families for the winter. It can get a little lonesome here in the winter time because of the wind, and snow that surrounds you. Do you think that would be a problem?"

Not really knowing what to say I just nodded that I would be fine and shrugged what really I knew about snow I was from Puerto Rico the island where snow never appeared.

33

The three of us went to where I would be staying in a big farm house or should I say camp house there was a section where eight men could sleep. The beds were made up of government army cots not the most comfortable piece of furniture to sleep on but it would have to do. Ramon handed me a blanket that had the appearance of the dirt outside wondering to myself if it had ever been washed. I would worry about that later. One thing I was relieved to see was the bathroom was fully equipped with a shower, toilet, and sink. No more running outside in the dead of night if I had to go. The rest of the building had a lot of windows a concrete floor and an old ancient stove but worked well as long as it worked. This building was heated but not greatly.

Outside were a lot of smaller houses for those that came back during the summer time and had more workers. These were scattered through out the campgrounds. I was a little worried about being alone with just a small staff of people myself the owners and, fifteen, workers. The day started at seven am and we worked in the packing house until five in the afternoon. What would happen is the machines would weigh and bag sacks of three pound increments of onions. My job was to stack the onions on a wooden pallet until I had forty bags there and keep them moving. Monotonous and cold. The packing house was not heated all of this was done in the winter inside but still cold. This went on for six days a week. At times I really thought that maybe I was going to freeze to death getting use to the harsh winters of upstate New York was not easy to do. Occasionally there was Carlos who would show up at the camp and sell second hand clothing for a dollar I made sure and bought this long brown coat before anyone else. The thing I liked about this particular coat was that it reached to my knees and kept most of me warm.

Snow finally fell white fluffy stuff very beautiful to see when it falls through the night sky. Clean and, fresh smelling. I wonder if you have ever noticed the smell of snow I know that there is a smell to it. It has a fresh air sort of smell to it. I also got sooo quiet after it fell and yes it was beautiful and silent. I felt a little alone but I also started feel a sense of mending after all of the previous beatings I had to endure at the hands of my father whom I usually refer to as the octopus.

After some time summer was coming and I notice that the farm started to come alive with so many more people showing up from all kinds of places.

I noticed some strange things also started to happen on this particular farm and in this particular time. I had made it to the summer of 1970 and it seemed that there was a bus load of women that appeared every Saturday night. I thought

"Maybe it was because we were all paid Saturday and these strange ladies of the night knew this."

I later found out that there were managed what some one would call a pimp interesting. Once in a while a load of eight or more would show up some even sporting black eyes and missing teeth.

I never really had much use for this type of lady maybe it is just me but seeing my fellow workers having a hard time peeing afterwards just sort of turned my stomach. I mean come on wouldn't it turn yours. I guess some of them were pretty enough I had the thought of how many men they had before me and the smell of one of them almost killed me once and all she did was remove her underwear. Along with the ladies drug dealers would show up with the choice of heroine, cocaine or marijuana. I watched as men my age older and younger abuse themselves with these things later not able to pee or holding their stomachs as if they were on fire I just never got the draw. Why would a man make himself sick on purpose? One thing I think that bothered me the most out of all of this was it all happened right before my eyes and I had to live with these men.

"Can you imagine shoving something into your veins with a needle that is not clean or sterile why?

Gambling would begin with a group of men either playing cards or shooting dice usually a fight would break out and grown men would try to fight each other to the death over a few dollars

"How stupid is that I ask?"

I don't know how or why but I managed to work at that farm for four years straight. Over the years there of going into town sometimes I made friends with two men on another farm called the Brown farm. This was another dirt farm that also produced onions it was run by two brothers Mickey and Barney Brown They were twin brothers of Polish descent, with a short stocky build just picture a pit-bull with a mans face.

They were all business never joking or cracking a smile. They were constantly fighting with each other though the workers had all kinds of nicknames for them.

One the hens of Brown. If they only knew, what we called them, behind their backs. This farm had fewer workers than the Grass farm they had about forty workers if that. The workers were from Mexico men and women some black men from the southern states and a few people from Puerto Rico.

The house they had was so much nicer with new kitchen appliances and the bed was a lot better than the farm prior. Every morning we all loaded onto the school bus and went out into the fields to pick the weeds from the onions. This was Monday through Saturday from seven AM. Until late every afternoon. By the end of October a lot of workers left and went back to their family. I was determined never to go back to Puerto Rico where the octopus lived although I did miss my other family members from time to time.

In October just like the other farm the onions were packed in the packing house to my relief and comfort this packing house was heated. I worked at this farm for three years during my stay I did manage to make two friends Gravier, and Pedro. Gravier was 5'7" and light skin chewed tobacco al the time and was from Puerto Rico. One of the most notable characteristics of Gravier was how old he looked. It had to be due to working on the fields all of his life. Pedro was short and skinny he was one of the hardest workers I had ever seen and chained smoked boy did he chain smoke I asked him one day

"Hey Pedro, why don't you just stick, the whole pack of smokes, in your mouth, and light it at once? I think you would do better that way."

One Sunday I had some time and decided to go to the local supermarket the Big V in Florida NY and I met up with some other friends that I use to chat and spend some time with to pass the time They stayed at the Benjamin and Hector they stayed at the Seviche farm not to far from the farm I was at about a forty five minute on foot walking at regular speed. One weekend, on my way back, from spending time, with Hector and Benjamin. I noticed a police cruiser speeding by me I did not take any notice of it until I passed the house that the police car had stopped at. There was a lady on the front porch now pointing and yelling in my direction

"He did it that's him. He is the one. Why don't you go and arrest him!"

The police officer on her stoop answered her abruptly

"That guy was walking a mile up the road back that way when I was coming to your home. There is no possibility he was the guy." The officer said and spit on the ground shaking his head as if to not believe how stupid this lady was.

As I passed by I realized that this young officer was not going to do something just because someone pointed a finger.

I worked at the Brown farms for a stretch of three years and started to get tired of this life. I wondered what maybe Little town would have in store for me. Watching all of my coworkers either getting hooked on drugs gambling, or women started to have an ill effect on me and I knew in my heart that it was time for me to find something better for myself.

CHAPTER 11

Judy's Bar

On the corner of North street and Wiser Avenue
In Little Town New York is Judy's bar. This was in a very prominent place at the time right by the main light and close enough to all of the daily activities in the town. Most would frequent this bar either after work in the many factories Little town had or to dance on the weekends. The bar had the shape of a triangle which would give its difference to others, or significance if you choose. It had the typical bar with stools and a window which anyone passing by could see who was inside at the bar. There was a single door to the building in the back. A couple of chairs sprinkled the dinning area where there was a rather small dance area and a juke box, a pool table and dart board on the back wall. The owner of the bar was Joe a big fat tall man that almost never frequented the bar. I think it played havoc on his sobriety.

Now Cecil was another story he was the bartender and who could not recognize him. He wore a large cowboy hat and sported a white shirt with a bow tie. Cecil was of Island descent and very rich dark skin and his voice was very distinctive loud and yes some would say obnoxious.

One night in early September I decided to go to Judy's bar after a heated argument with my girlfriend Christine to blow off some steam. I was there trying to get control of my emotions, and give, the, argument, a rest. I really do not know what the argument was about and really did not care. I was ready to relax and enjoy myself for a while with the other local's

"Hey Cecil what's new?" Just a sign of pleasantries I had learned with my new understanding of the English language which I was getting a little better at.

I order myself a beer from the tap since that was the cheapest way to go. The jukebox was on and some happy music was playing to my relief. Sometimes you would get a woman in there and well, if she had just broken up with a boyfriend, I along with everyone else would have to suffer through some tear jerking song over and over again. But not tonight, this night things were pretty laid back with a light atmosphere. I heard in the bar from the distance.

"Diego."

I ignored the person who was calling me. I was having too much fun talking and dancing a little and sporting a few mugs of beer.

"Diego come here." There it was again, who in the blazes was calling me? I looked around and kind of thought it was someone calling me from outside. I still did not get up, happy to be right where I am bopping to the new song on the jukebox now and cracking some dirty jokes with some people in the bar. After a few more minutes I turned my barstool around and I saw

Shorty standing behind me. Shorty's real name is Jose Colon but everyone called him Shorty which fits since he was extremely short and very thin almost gangly. I only knew him from working together in the black dirt farm in coldsnap New York; we only knew each other from that capacity.

"What the hell do you want?" I asked my intruding acquaintance.

Shorty answered in very low voice barley audible.

"I have a TV I want to give you."

"Why?" I asked him not really sure what he was talking about. And pissed off, for the intrusion.

"Where is it?" I asked him finally since he was still breathing down my neck and not moving. Disturbing.

"Outside, I tried to sell it but no one wants it I can't carry it home. It is pretty big too, can't you use a TV?"

Shorty finally finished his story.

I went outside where Shorty had the TV and two large black garbage bags filled not sure with what and at this point I really do not care. I poked my head into the bar

"Hey Cecil good night man see you next week."

Cecil nodded towards me and went about his business. I hoisted the TV on my shoulders and headed to where I lived which was only about three blocks if that. I knocked on the front door where my girlfriend and her mother lived. Christine opened the door.

"Where did that come from?" Christina asked

Looking at the TV I put on the floor.

"Shorty gave it to me. I guess he was to weak or stupid to take it to where he lived. I can hook it up in out room in the morning right now I am going to get some sleep."

....

Not too long after as I was sleeping two undercover police officers where knocking at the front door and apparently had pistols drawn. Christine was the one who answered the door.

"Can I help you?" Christina asked a little shaken at the sight of these two men at her front door first thing in he morning.

"What will the neighbors think?" Christina thought in her head.

One of the gentlemen in a suit asked.

"Is Diego here?"

Christina not knowing what this was about showed the two officers into the bedroom where I was sleeping.

I heard strangers in the room and quickly woke up and blinked my eyes to see two men dressed in suits.

"Diego, can you get up come with us?'

I got up quickly and dressed. One of the officers pointed to the TV that was on the floor.

"Where did you get his?"

"Shorty gave it to me but we are not friends." I answered; now starting to get a uneasy feeling about the stupid TV the asshole could not carry last night.

One of the men took the TV I had on the floor and put it into the trunk of the car they had drove to the house in. This was a blue unmarked car not the typical black and white car the local police used. It was a short drive to the police station in Little Town. This was a very small station and inside was a bright lighted room with chairs and an ashtray and some chairs and a table. I was ushered into one of the small rooms and waited alone while I contemplated the events of last night. One of the police officers poked his head in and asked

"Do you want a coffee?"

I politely shook my head yes, a little while had passed and the officer brought back for the three of us coffees and egg and cheese sandwiches from the local restaurant not too far away, the Coney Island restaurant. I saw on the floor in the room the two large garbage bags that Shorty had with him last night.

"Diego do you know who's stuff this is?"

I answered truthfully "I saw Shorty with it last night outside the bar."

"Jose told us that you were with him when he stole the two bags of cigarettes and canned food and the TV.

Can you explain why he would say that?"

"I explained that I saw Jose last night outside the bar where he gave me the TV but nothing more. I mentioned I did see the bags but never really bothered to ask Jose about them."

"I hate to tell you this Diego but since you had stolen property in your possession and it is in conjunction with a robbery breaking and entering we have to charge you with a felony."

I was now feeling pretty upset about this knowing that something as stupid as taking a stolen TV would change my life dramatically. I started to feel I am not sure

"Anger, worry?"

A little time passed and I was before the Judge I was given the charge of felony robbery and was handed a get out of jail free bond of $2,500 money that would take me a whole year working on the field to make. I had to take the sentence instead. I was sent to Orange County Jail in Gosh New York. This is where you go for small crimes or first time offenders that did something small or would only have a year stay or less.

I was driven to the jail with my hands cuffed in front of me due to the fact of my nature was respectful and I was just going to do what I needed to get my time done and out of this mess thanks to Shorty.

"Asshole" I thought to myself on the ride to Gosh.

After my finger printing and mug shots I was interviewed by the fattest nurse I had ever seen. She was surprise and delighted to know how healthy I was. I just could not fly, I managed to tell her. When I was done with the nurse I was handed a plastic mattress for my bed. I changed into long pants and a blue shirt which was the uniform for small potato crimes like mine. People staying for a year or less. As I was walking down the hallway I saw men chained to one another with chains around their waist and hands and feet. As I walked down the hallway I spotted Shorty standing there against the wall hanging on to some of the rod iron bars. He saw me and his eyes got as big as saucers as he saw me and he put a stupid shit eating grin on his face. After I put my plastic mattress in my cell I quietly walked over to Shorty.

"You are a big freaking liar. Why did you tell them I helped you? I should break your fucking neck right now you little nothing but a fucking liar! Then I won't have to see your butt ugly face. everyday!" I said exasperated.

"Because of you asshole, I lose everything. You have nothing to lose do ya?"

Shorty did not answer but put his head down when I was done speaking to him. I walked away and went to my cell #14 saying under my breath.

"Asshole not, worth my time."

Time moves very slow in any type of jail situation. One day Christina came to visit me.

"Christina I don't want to be a problem for you just hold my clothes and forget about me. When I am done here I will just stop by and get my clothes. Thank you for caring and stopping and thank your mother Geraldine for letting me stay there."

I managed to keep myself as busy as anyone that has to do time and four months passed. I was brought to the Supreme Court to here my case. Abraham was the judge.

The judge looked at me and asked.

"Mr. Hillside, how do you feel?"

I answered "Your honor I feel bad because I do not like being locked up. It is a headache."

The judge read me the charge.

"I don't have anything to say to that. I had the TV Jose Colon gave me. He and I have never been friends I only saw him that night. I was minding my own business."

My public defender spoke up before the judge could say anything else.

"Hmm your honor can I speak to you in private?"

Not much time passed and the public defender and the judge returned. He put his arm around me and whispered in my ear.

"If you plead guilty the judge is willing to give you five years probation and you can go today."

I plead guilty.

CHAPTER 12

Elba Margarita

Winter of 79 I found myself moving into the life of father and husband. I really liked the quiet life and the thought of being a family man now.

Elba Margarita was the name of my beautiful bouncing baby girl. Surprising enough she was born the day after my birthday January 18, what a beautiful birthday present. She was born 8 lbs and 11 oz a perfect size she had all of her fingers and toes. Light brown skin like mine. And beautiful big brown eyes that lit up when she saw my face. What a joy that is. As I expected every inch of her like most parents do. I noticed she had the exact same birthmark as mine. It is the shape of heart perfect in dimension that clinched that real fact that she was mine.

As I cuddled her to my shoulder and patted her tiny back I cooed to her and made promises that only a father could make

"I am going to protect you and keep you safe. I want you to have pretty dresses and beautiful dollies just like you."

My marriage to Linda was not perfect and I thought perhaps because she was so young and inexperienced.

Not long ago I lost my job due to her constant calling the job site to ask for me. Talk about being worried about my every move, almost like someone suffocating another with love. It can feel very uncomfortable. I now had a job in Coldsnap New York where they make dirty magazines you know the kind dirty old men buy. To look at vaginas and boobs of all sizes. It was a job for now and paid the rent and bills. I hated leaving my daughter every morning with my mother in law. I did not like her and she did not like me so you could say the feeling was mutual. She was constantly calling names like nigger and other things that just did make any sense. Not long after Linda was pregnant her own mother started trouble with us by saying that the baby wasn't mine. Who would do something like that? what a witch. But the heart shape birthmark proved to me that my mother in law was insane.

I was at work and I noticed black shadows swirling around and making sure that I would see them. Looking around to make sure no one saw me acting nuts by paying attention to these shadows. I had the strangest feeling that something terrible is about to happen or it already had. This happened on Friday the end of the week. My friend was kind enough to give me a ride home from Coldsnap to Little Town where we lived and I could not shake that dreaded feeling. As we pulled into the driveway where I lived there was Linda and my mother in-law. I thought to myself

"This crazy fucking old woman I bet has left Elba alone. I am going to ask the old witch where she is as soon as I get out of this car."

"Jenny where is Elba? Is she in the house?"

Jenny answered me rolling her eyes

"No Elba is at my house, she should be all right. What are you getting so nervous for?"

"Let's go now I don't want to waste time." I yelled not too happy with my mother in law or my wife what were they retarded? I was starting to have my doubts about this entire family but I kept my cool in the car as she drove to her house. While Jenny drove I kept my mouth shut. Jenny was an elderly woman that was constantly smoking and had long grey pony tail God how I hated that woman. I only tolerated her because my own family was too far away to ask for help. We all rode in silence as I fumed hoping and praying that everything was all right. We pulled into the driveway and I knew not only did she not have any clues on how to act; she always kept her front door open I got out of the car and quickly went inside. There she was on the master bed covered with a blue and white knitted blanket and obviously had been crying for a long time. Elba's coloring on her face was black or blue like someone that was having a hard time catching there breath she was only five months and left alone for twenty five miles to my home and twenty five miles back. Not knowing how soon she left so I could really only gather that the baby was left along for an hour or more.

Later at home

"Linda I don't think that your mother is the best person to watch our daughter. I want you to quit your job at the hospital and stay home with her. What would you have done if something had happened to her? I mean really is working that important to you? You never liked to work when we were together what has changed now?"

Linda just sat there looking at me like a big fat dummy not really understanding how dangerous leaving the baby with Jenny really was. Nothing changed and I kept on working in Coldsnap and Linda kept on working at the hospital and Jenny my mother in law kept watching the baby. I hated going to work but really had no other choice in the matter. I made more money than my wife so I was the one that had to work.

Late in May I saw those shadows again while I was at work and it made me very nervous. I was desperate to get home because I remembered what had happened before when I saw those shadow figures. This was Friday and everyone of course got paid, so the day was long and for me the ride was just as long as the day

When we approached my home my brother was there. Daren, he lived in the city and had obviously taken the Short Line bus from the city to Little town. He had been doing that lately because he had a girl in town he was dating, no one permanent just a friend he would go and hang out with at the local bars.

"Hey how are you? How is everyone in New York?"

Daren answered "everyone is the same nothing new really."

We went inside and sat down at the kitchen table

"You know something really weird has been happening. Today more than the other days I saw black creepy shadows everywhere while I was at work. I was the only one that sees them and I have a terrible feeling about something. The last time I saw these shadows my daughter was alone screaming and I had the same dreadful feelings in the pit of my stomach. I just can't explain it."

"Shadows?" My brother answered, trying to understand.

"Do you want some coffee?"

"Can we get a six pack of beer I need to get cigarettes too do you mind?"

"No that is fine the store down the street sells beer and we can get your cigarettes there. Let me just use the bathroom first and we can walk there give me a couple of minutes."

"Okay I will wait for you outside on the front step."

I went to the bathroom grabbed my keys to the door and twenty dollars. I figured that would be enough for a six pack of beer and a pack or two for my brother.

"Have you heard from Puerto Rico?" I asked my brother as we walked back making small chatter.

"Evy called the house the other day and we spoke to her and, Poppy, nothing new over there." Answered Daren.

In the kitchen I pulled the tab on my can of beer and sat down at the kitchen table.

"Knock knock"

I could have sworn I heard someone knocking on the door. We kept on discussing nothing important. Mostly Puerto Rico and family and making stupid jokes as brother's do.

"Knock, knock, knock," I heard it again

"Dario quiet a minute did you hear that?"

"What?"

"knock, knock, knoc, rap, rap, rap,"

My brother and I looked at each other.

"Let me go see who it is at the door." Leaving the kitchen to answer the door.

Daren, not too far behind me. Opening the door was a young police officer with long auburn her and with a very solemn look to her.

"Now what" I thought to my self.

"Are you Diego? Can you come with me?"

Not sure what was going on. Since she, did not crack out the handcuffs for me. I realized that something just was not right. I decided to ask the young female office.

"Can my brother come with me?"

"Yes he can ride in the back and Diego you can ride in the front if you want."

The ride was very quiet, no small talk. The officer chose to not speak. I don't know why but it felt as if time stood still during that ride. I recognized the street we were going on and it was no where close to the police station and we were traveling up the steep hill. The hospital on the hill, Horton Memorial hospital is the only hospital in Little town. My palms were starting to sweat; I could feel my heart beating and could here my brother's every breath. The officer got out of the car and opened the door for me and my brother. We went inside the front door to the hospital. A nurse was waiting for us. She had a name badge that said Toby and long blond hair and very thin but something in her face told me that something was very wrong.

"Mr. Hillside my name is Toby and I am the nurse supervisor to the hospital. I have some very bad news to tell you and this may come as a shock. Can I get you some water?"

Just shaking my head no. Toby continued.

"Is this family with you?" I could only nod a response. I was too frozen to sound audible.

"Your daughter Elba was brought here a while ago and we did everything possible to save her. When she arrived she was very cyanotic which means it was apparent that she was struggling for a breath. The Er Dr. did what is known as infant chest palpations on her little chest and tried to revive her. After thirty minutes or more on an infant your daughter's size it's very difficult to have a survival rate. Your daughter died about forty five minutes ago."

The young nurse was telling me all of this and I only heard a word or two the shadows I had been seeing all along were trying to warn me. Why did I not pay attention?

"Please come with me Diego." The nurse headed to the examining room where my little daughter lay on the examining table bare-chested with her Pampers on her.

I walked over to her and picked her up and held her little body to my chest. Not feeling anything at this time

Only the little girl I loved so much lifeless in my arms.

I caressed her beautiful face and told my Elba

"My precious little girl. I love you with all my heart."

The tears quietly rolled down my face, burning a hole in my heart. Knowing I was having this last few moments with Elba.

"I love you more than my own life if God would have it I would take your place. But it appears that this is not possible. I want you to know that your daddy loves you with all of his heart. You were the reason I changed my ways and became a better man. For that my beautiful baby I thank you. I will always keep you in my heart. I will never pass one day without thinking about you. I have to give you to God and the angels, to watch over you, keep you safe in heaven. I love you my beautiful girl." The tears kept falling and I could feel myself trying hard to breathe my self.

I knew that moment what real despair was. I laid my little on down on the examining table and motioned for the nurse to come in the room.

"Diego is there anything you want the hospital to do before you make arrangements?"

Knowing in my heart that I suspected my mother in law Jenny of doing something to my daughter, I asked the hospital to perform an autopsy. Daren entered the room now where I had laid my daughter down and put his arm around me to comfort me. Words did not come from him. Having my brother there was a help, Daren sensed that this was not the time for jokes or games and just stayed quiet. My brother and I left the room where my daughter lay. Walking to the main entrance of the hospital there is a circular drive to drop off expectant mothers, people getting blood test, and chairs that held the different patients and families as they waited to be registered into the hospital.

My mother in-law was there with her two daughters, my sister in laws Jessie and Rita. Before I knew it Jenny sucker punched me and hit me right behind my ear with her fist. It landed pretty hard. I was not in the mood to be a gentle man right now and I hit her back. The girls were now swinging their pocketbooks and hitting me as much as they could. Daren got in the middle trying to separate all of us.

"Have some fucking respect he just lost his daughter!!!"

"Hey someone help me. This man is attacking me!"

Yelled Jenny.

"I don't think so I saw the whole thing. And I know you hit him first I was sitting right here when you swung at this man that did nothing to you. I am calling the police and you will be the one they bring in. Not him I will make sure of it, and for your information madam. the hospital has video footage of this area of the hospital so the film showing you striking this man first.

It will be enough to haul your fat ass away. I can guarantee it. Now get out of here and take your ugly daughters with you." The nurse that came to my defense was red in the face now, shaking with anger.

The next day .... I went back to the hospital and asked them at the front where my daughter was.

"Excuse me. My daughter died here yesterday. Can you tell me where I can find her?"

The receptionist nodded her head and typed a few things on her computer. "One minute sir let me make a call to double check. I do not want to send you to the wrong place. Usually the deceased is brought to a funeral home. We have more than one we use here at the hospital, just give me a few minutes and I will get you the name of the funeral home and address." The receptionist got up and went to the inner office and made a call. I could faintly hear what she was saying, and returned to the desk where I was sitting.

"Mr. Hillside your daughter is at the Morse funeral home on North Street, here on the corner of North and Grand Street. Are you familiar with that area?"

"Yes miss thank you for your help."

She was wearing a beautiful green dress and little white socks with lace that had a hint of green to match the dress she was wearing. The stitches from the autopsy on her forehead were visible. Looking into the little casket I touched her little arms and gave her a photo of me holding her. This way she would know that I loved her even in heaven when she arrived. She looked like a small child's little doll as she laid there in her child size light blue casket with white silk to frame her little body and face. The service was held at St. Andrews church on Grand Street. The only people at the service for my daughter was me my wife and Daren that day. I had made it very clear that I did not want any family there other than that. The service was like any other funeral service.

Elba Margarita

Born Jan 18, 79 Died May 79

CHAPTER 13

Christmas Eve

I was still grieving over my daughter Elba and really not in the mood to celebrate Christmas. Linda was grumpy and a little upset about me wanting to just stay at peace and not celebrate Christmas this year.

She was invited to a party and was itching to go. I really could not understand why she was already willing o celebrate.

"Linda if you want to go to your family go. I won't stop you. But I am not in the mood for any type of party."

Linda left. I passed the day alone. I decided to go to the church where my daughter lay and tell her how much I missed her. It was cold but I put on a wind breaker jacket and jeans and sneakers and went up to the church where Elba was buried. It was later in the morning and not too much activity going on in the town.

Kneeling down at my daughter's grave I pulled some weeds and made her area a little neater. As I was praying I noticed a beautiful woman in a red dress. I could smell her. She smelled of beautiful flowers that bloom in the spring time. She passed by me ever so gracefully and said

"I see your child. She has beautiful happy smile on her face."

Just as quick as the lady in red said that, I looked back to reply but she vanished. For some reason unknown to me she gave me a gentle good feeling. That maybe the angels are watching out after my daughter. I planted some bulbs that I brought with me so I could find her marking in the spring. We did not have a headstone for Elba just a round circle with her number. She was in a area they reserved for children that passed.

I went back home and Linda was there getting ready to leave for her family.

"Diego are your sure you want to stay here all by yourself? It might not be a bad idea to get out among other people."

I just nodded no to reconfirm my not wanting to socialize. While Linda was out I cleaned the tiny apartment and decided to cook something for us for dinner. It gave me time to reflect on the lady in the cemetery and things that had passed. Jenny returned home about eleven pm. My neighbor had earlier invited me to a party which I did not go to. They were not to keen on my wife, since Linda had a bad habit of starting trouble all the time. Linda was jealous of Isabelle.

"I have food here if you want to eat." I exclaimed since I was tired from waiting for my wife I decided to lay down in bed. Linda soon came into the bed very short after me. Out of nowhere I could feel Linda put a vise grip around my testicles and held on.

"What the hell is a matter with you? Let go of me!!!"

She continued to hold on and started to squeeze even tighter. All I could do was try and think of a way to get her from hanging onto my balls. I balled my hand into a fist and knuckled her as hard as I could into her eye until she let go. The pain was excruciating. I limped out into the kitchen in a rage and ready to kill her right then, in there looking for a something in the kitchen; I grabbed a big sharp knife. A voice appeared out of no where.

"Don't kill her, go!"

Knowing that the voices I had heard before had saved me I grabbed my jeans, shoes and light jacket and put the knife in my pocket just in case she came after me.

Where was I to go this was Christmas Eve and late at night. I had no money and I knew I had friends in Orange, Benjamin and Hector. I knew I had to leave to save myself from destruction and from becoming a killer. It was cold but the burning I felt between my legs from Linda's assault on me made it hard to concentrate on anything else.

It had begun to snow. I walked down Academy avenue and onto Dolson Avenue and the wind started to pick up and so did the snow now falling a lot faster and sticking to the ground. Gradually the snow turned into freezing rain but I was determined to get to Orange Island it was a sixteen mile walk and these weather conditions made it worse.

My ears started to feel numb. I noticed that I did not feel my toes now frozen inside my sneakers. I kept on walking determined that the voice I heard would guide me.

I managed to get on route 17 this is a back country road where houses were far from one another and it was mostly in a wooded area. No signs of any path in the road, my walk had suddenly become very torturous. I was starting to get a terrible feeling that I may die out here walking in the freezing rain I started to get very thirsty and my hair had frozen over. I felt my legs getting heavier and heavier and finding it very difficult to walk. Since it was Christmas Eve there were no lights on anywhere or across on this back road either. I noticed in the distance a light on in a barn. I knew there were cows there because I had passed this barn on other occasions. I knocked on the barn door.

"Hello, hello anyone here. I need help I just need something to drink. Anyone here? I have been walking all night and my hair and everything else is frozen. Hello?"

There was no one here but the cattle. I noticed right away how warm the barn felt compared to the outdoors.

I looked around still to see if anyone was there. The owners were across the street. I took off my shoes and jacket and put them by the boiler to dry. I walked quietly over to the milk container and drank three pans. I thought to myself

"Oh God I am not going to freeze to death."

The cows looked at me as almost as if they knew I was not there to harm them. They moved over to make room for me and I slid down the side of the barn and fell asleep sitting up.

I was wearing a watch with a light on it five am. I opened my eyes just for a moment and fell back to sleep again feeling the warmth and the safety of the barn. I felt something tapping my shoulder, it took me a minute to realize I was not dreaming and in fact someone was actually tapping me to wake up. It was a police officer.

"What are you doing here?" He quietly asked me.

"I had a fight with my wife and I did not want to kill her so I took what clothes I had on my back and left. I have two friends at the Tesoviechi farm in Orange Island and I was trying to walk there. It started to snow and rain I was worried I was going to die on the back roads from the weather and the walk I was taking." I quickly explained to the police officer that had his full attention on my story.

"I have to arrest you for criminal trespassing. The owner called and said you were sleeping in his barn."

I got up and dressed with my now warm and dry clothing and I noticed when the police officer opened the door to the out side, it looked like we were in Alaska. There were no signs of any life at all just snow. I quietly wondered how the officer made it out here without wearing snow shows or using a snow blower.

Since I was probably of no threat the officer cuffed me in front and escorted me to the car. He drove to the Monty State Police office. This office sits out on the highway all by its self like a sore thumb. They did the usual booking procedure finger prints and mug shots. Getting back in the cruiser, we headed to the Orange County Court house in Gosh New York I only waited about ten minutes for the judge. I was the only person that day to face a judge it was quick. The judge asked me if I was able to post a 500.00 bail to get out. I was not and the judge said

"I will see you in ten days."

I then left and went to the orange county jail. The following day there was an article in the paper with my name on it saying I had sex with a cow. How insane was that. I would have had to use a stool or have a running leap to reach her to have sex with her. What people put in papers was very strange. The tenth day arrived and I was in court in front of the same judge as before.

"I can let you go Diego I do not believe for a second the stuff they added here it would be very interesting though if it was the truth. But in my mind I find it impossible for that to be true. The police officer that arrested you told the court that he found you sleeping on the barn floor anyway. I know you would have to be super human to have sex with those cows."

CHAPTER 14

The drive

Six months later I found myself living in Newt. When I arrived there the first thing I did was purchase the Times Herald Record. This is one of the most popular papers of the Orange County area. I scanned the ads looking for rooms to rent. Luckily I noticed one and decided to give it a try, what did I have to lose?

I walked to the hotel on Grand Street. The building was on the banks of the Hudson River it was about six stories high made of concrete brick and looked from the street to be an old building. I went inside to the office and politely asked

"Hello, is the manager here?"

A tall skinny man was standing by the window and turned around. He had on an absurd yellow wig not blonde but a cheap yellow one that looked like it was made for a big doll.

"That's me"

The tall skinny man answered, and smiled. Lord almighty, he not only had a head of yellow gold, he had a mouth of yellow gold to match from ear to ear. I have to say that is the most gold I ever saw in my life in one place. And it was in this man's mouth.

"My name is Lenny. Would you like to go up and check the room we have empty on the sixth floor?"

"Sure." Thinking the manager would escort me he did not but handed me a key to room #208.

"Just go down the hallway to the elevator go to the sixth floor you will find that room up there." Lenny handed me the key and continued to watch out the window in his office at the river where the shipping boats were passing by.

I walked down the hallway with the key to the room in hand. I came to the elevator.

"Now how does this machine work I wonder?"

I thought to my self and pushed the two buttons and the doors squealed open.

I noticed it was like a traveling hallway. Very strange I had never seen one before. I walked into the moving hallway box and looked at the panel with buttons I had no idea at the time I only needed to push the button that said number six. Instead I pushed every button and hoped for the best.

The elevator shook like there was an earthquake and made a lot of noise. I was a little scared at first but glad I made t safely to the sixth floor. After my interesting ride in the elevator I made it to the room.

It was small with two windows one by the front and one on the side. Out of one of the windows I could see the Hudson River. What a beautiful sight seeing the river and boats of grandeur.

The room was furnished with a twin bed a small closet and little night stand. There was brown carpet. The room was neat and clean and the bathroom had all the things necessary to wash and relieve my self if I had to go. It wasn't fancy but it would do for me.

I walked down the hallway to the earth quaking elevator where a little black girl held it open for me and proceeded down to the first floor I watched what she did so I would not end up on all six floors.

I went back to the office and spoke to Lenny the golden man about the rent and gave him 200 dollars for the month.

My first night at the hotel was just as interesting as my first ride in the elevator. I did not have any radio or TV to keep me occupied to waste away the time. I laid down my weary bones and reflected on the past and grateful that I had a safe place to live. Noticing the time on my wristwatch seven pm I decided it wouldn't hurt to get a much needed good nights rest. This was of course so much better than a jail cell. Or even in the same apartment with Linda. I drifted off to sleep.

"Whoooot! Whooot,! Whoot whoot.,"

A large cargo ship was passing in the river and making it known to all that it was there. I had never heard that noise before and thought perhaps the hotel was on fire. Not wasting anytime I grabbed my t-shirt jeans and sneakers and fled down to the bottom floor and went outside.

Not seeing anyone else. Besides me standing outside in the middle of the night. Made me wonder what the devil was going on here. I glanced at my watch and saw it was 4:30 am.

"Whooot, Whoot,"

There it went again. I realized it was just a large ship passing by. I decided to stay awake. Going down to the lobby early to grab a cup of coffee. I decided to walk to the big church I had noticed earlier.

The church was on Grand Street I introduced myself to the Reverend and his wife. I mentioned that I was going to see if I could get work at a factory I saw in the paper on Jenny Drive. It was a factory that made beds from what I could gather from the ad I had read earlier and thought that would be a good place to start.

The Reverend knew the place I was talking about and gave me a ride there. I did manage to get the job the first time I went in and spoke to the foreman.

The ride over was about a half an hour. Knowing now where it was and about how long it took by car. I realized I had to get up pretty early the next day to make it to work on time.

The walk took about two hours or so. Luckily I made friends with a very nice black woman who worked at the same place and lived very close to the hotel. She had seen me walking a lot and realized who I was and we made a deal. She drove me back and forth to work and I paid her for gas fifteen dollars every paycheck for the favor. A lot of the men at the factory and people in general didn't like her because she was a lesbian I just thought she was nice and never gave her sexual orientation another thought.

..........six months later..............

Around July I was watching the boats from my window I heard what I thought was knocking.

I ignored it because I had no friends here in Newt and continued in my own thoughts watching the boats out the river.

"Knock, Knock," silence then a little faster and louder

"KNOCK! KNOCK! KNOCK!"

I opened the door and in front of me stood Linda .....I could not believe my eyes there she stood right there.

"Who told you I was living here?" I asked her now exasperated and silently wishing her dead.

Linda smiled at me with her stupid grin and said

"My girlfriend Patty told me."

I thought to myself "She must have really good spies."

I never told anyone where I was and Linda was the last person I wanted to see ever.

"Patty told me you lived in this hotel. I spoke to that ugly man downstairs with the gold teeth that you're my husband and I wanted to know what room you were in. He gave me your room number."

"I didn't forget Christmas Eve when you started your crap with squeezing my balls. Because of you I chose to be as far away from you as possible, you are real lucky to be alive. So... What the hell do you want?"

I asked Linda now wishing more than ever she would just leave me alone.

Linda answered "we are still married you know. I'm going to stay here."

"You can't stay here the owner's won't like it because I never mentioned you to anyone. You can just stay tonight but tomorrow I am going to visit Little town to see my daughter. It is has been a while I want you out of here tomorrow." I said without getting emotional with her or losing my temper.

The next day came and Linda and I were walking to the bus terminal. As Linda and I walked in silence. we heard a car beeping over and over a blue Chevy car pulled up beside us. A little dark skin man rolled with his window rolled down asked.

"Do you know where Little town is?"

"Yes we are going there now, why?"

The man then said

"I will give you a ride there since we are all going the same way. You don't mind do ya?"

"Okay" I answered and Linda and I got in the car.

"Hey man, my name is Diego, can you drop her off at her mothers first?" I asked the man without introducing my wife.

Just knowing I could rid myself of her was enough to make me happy that day.

"Sure man by the way my name is Miguel Rodriguez"

"Hey Miguel, do you work around here?"

"Yeah I work at Majestic factory on not too far from here."

We made it to Little town and dropped Linda off to her families' house. I thought to myself that perhaps this would be a good opportunity to go to Pine Cone and see friends of mine. That is if Miguel was up to it. I figured I could visit Elba's grave another time.

"Do you know Orange? I have a lot of friends down there in the camps and today would be a good day to visit because they all have to day off."

Miguel looked at me and then answered

"No problem lets go, you show me the way."

We got to Orange and visited with my friends we laughed and had a good ole boys day of it. Eating and drinking telling stories and joking around when I decided to look at my watch and saw it was going to be one am. Soon and I had to get up in a few hours to be at work.

"Hey, Miguel come on let's go I have to be to work soon and it is late."

We got in the car and Miguel left the driveway where we were I noticed that he was a little lead footed when he pulled out.

"Hey, I know these roads better than you. Slow down because some turns are hard to handle even when you are driving slow sometimes."

Ignoring what I had said he pushed his foot on the gas and was moving at a dangerously high speed for this part of the area. Orange has many back curvy roads and usually there is not too much traffic, just because of that these particular roads where known not to be the safest route to take when you were going at a faster rate of speed. Many of the roads wind around or have hairpin turns some if you not careful could end you up in a ditch or face to face with a rock wall.

"Hey you need to slow down to make the left up here or your going to hit the wall."

Before I got the word out of my mouth we were heading straight for the rock wall with no time to slow or stop. Miguel tried to late to manipulate the car to come to a slower speed, the car spun around in rotation three or four times before landing hard onto the rock wall pinning me inside the car. The car was smashed in on my side.

I tried to move my self to get out and saw that my leg was badly hurt and mangled. After I tried this I muttered out loud

"I am going to die"

No sooner did I say these words did I see Miguel get out of the car without a scratch and looked like he was not worried about leaving me there to die.

At the moment I felt no pain and knew enough by looking at my leg that I was badly hurt. A man and a woman that lived close by came out of there house after hearing the noise and the man asked me

"Are you hurt?" He asked looking into the car.

He turned around and told his wife to go back and call an ambulance and the police. He opened the driver side of the car and managed to pull me out of the car by grabbing me from under my armpits. He did this ever so carefully and laid me onto the ground out of the road and close to the car.

Usually there is no traffic on this part of the road but tonight there were drivers that stopped and asked if they could be of service and were told by the man who pulled me out that an ambulance was on the way. One of the people that had stopped to see if they could help and left their car running out of the blue.

He screamed "Hey that guy just stole my car!"

It was Miguel who got me into this mess. He had stolen the car from the people that had stopped and got out of their car to help. Through all the commotion I could see my leg was twisted, really badly disfigured.

The ambulance came and put me on a stretcher and drove me to Horton Memorial emergency room in Little town New York. I was put in a room with so much pain and had to endure it what seemed to be forever apparently there was orthopedic surgeon at the hospital and there I waited in the worst pain in my life. Praying that I wouldn't die before the doctor came, the nurses and orderlies did not give me any pain meds and flat out refused them to me.

Finally the orthopedic came inside and shook my hand

"Hello I am Dr. Martin I know that you have a broken leg."

As the Dr. said that he grabbed my broken leg pulled it into the right position grabbed a drill, made holes through my thigh bone put in a metal plate and hung weight on the end of my leg and lifted it up with a pulley.

This was all done so quickly, in a matter of minutes thank God otherwise I think the ordeal would have killed me for sure if he had done this slower.

"Your leg is going to be pretty swollen over the next few weeks, before I can do anything else move it a little bit like this"

He motioned with his hand to not put me in anymore pain then needed.

"Don't worry you are going to be alright your going to have pain though so I am giving you Morphine to help."

I laid there after the Dr. left for a good long time before an orderly came and drove my bed up to the fifth floor.

After the orderlies left I could see out of my hospital window that the Orange County Fair was in progress I could see the light to the Ferris wheel from my bed.

CHAPTER 15

The Hospital

I laid there with my leg up in the air feeling like a trussed pig. The pain was unbearable at times, if it wasn't for the morphine shots I don't think I could have borne it.

Mimi was the nurse who usually came in everyday to check on me. She was very nice, a little young blonde with a very sweet sounding voice. I think since I was one of the patients that complained the least she had a soft place for me. As I lay in the hospital as it's guest everyday like clockwork right around dinner time,

Linda would appear. I don't know if she came to see me or if she was more interested in eating my dinner. I swear it was as if she never ate anything in her life. And like clock work after she gobbled down her share of my food she would start some of the stupidest arguments.

"I mean really how can a person find stupid things to argue about over nothing?"

One evening I got disgusted with watching her wolf down my food I asked her.

"Are you here to see me or my dinner?"

I looked at her with my eyebrows knitted together to let her know I was not impressed with her coming everyday to either start trouble or to just sit there like a big dummy. Linda looked at me and was pissed and stood up and said rather loudly for all the hospital to hear

"I hope you drop dead you mother fucker!!"

Mimi came in the room shaking her head

"Hey quiet down you this is a hospital not romper room!"

Mimi was tough she stood there tapping her one foot looking straight at my wife. Linda grabbed her purse flung it over her shoulder and stomped out. I buzzed for the nurse to come in my room.

"Is there anyway I can keep Linda my wife out of my room? I really don't get any rest when she is here and all she does is fight with me. I know you were here earlier when she started in on me."

"Yes, Diego we can arrange for her not to visit. I will let security downstairs know, is that all right?"

Plumping my pillow a little I had time to think to myself now that I had no interference.

"I would recover. This is just a temporary set back."

I think after I reflected a little while the pain medication was starting to work and I drifted off to sleep. I wasn't sure if I was dreaming or if it was real but I heard a familiar voice.

"Diego, Diego,"

I fluttered my eyes a little to make sure there was no one in my room but the voice was all too familiar it sounded like my moms voice. I had not seen her since I left Puerto Rico over fourteen years ago. Can this be real is this really her in my room or am I hallucinating the voice I so longed to hear from time to time?"

Forcing myself awake fully there she was in the flesh my mother Moya standing in my room wiping her eyes and muttering to herself

"This isn't Diego it can't be he looks so pale and little."

"Ma hey don't worry I am okay. I was just in a car accident, that's all. The doctor is going to do surgery when the swelling goes down and then I'll be fine.

I won't be here forever." I said trying to comfort my mother who looked more delicate than I did.

"Diego your cousins are here and my niece and nephew we all came down from the city to see you but the guard at the door to the hospital said you were in critical condition and I was the only one that was allowed to see you."

"Mom I really don't need any visitors. I will be fine, please don't worry you can tell everyone that I am fine and just need my rest."

My mother stayed a short time that afternoon since there was a van load of people waiting for her downstairs she kissed me on my cheek

"Dios Bendiga" and quietly left my room.

Linda would call from time to time and beg to come and visit. I finally let in and reminded her that she was not to come for my dinner it was mine to eat and to not start any trouble. She agreed and returned to visit me again.

The only bright time to my days of lying in bed like a trussed up pig was when Nancy came everyday to straighten up my room and clean. She was a cute little thing with brown curly hair and brown eyes and such a cute little smile that she looked like a doll at times. Nancy would stay and we would talk about nothing and I sensed that Nancy was starting to get a crush on me.

"I can come back later and visit if you want?" Nancy said to me with here eyes bright like an eager puppy.

I hated to tell her this but I had to.

"No, Nancy don't come here later that is when my wife usually comes and she is the size of a football player big and with a big mouth."

I didn't want that for my new friend I had that brightened my days here in Horton hospital.

"I know Linda would find a way to start trouble with you so please do not come at night okay I look forward to seeing you in the morning anyway." I said trying hard to not hurt Nancy's feelings.

Dr. Martin would check my progress on my leg to see if the swelling had gone down enough to do surgery and the time had finally come. Dr. Martin said to me

"I think it's time Diego. The swelling has gone down enough for me to do surgery I need to put you back together. I need to explain what is going to happen. First you will be put under anesthesia and I will have to place pins in your leg. You broke it pretty bad in two places in the front and the back. You will wake with pins and a cast from your hip to your ankle. This is to make sure you keep your leg still as it heals. Now I need to warn you when you wake up you will be in more pain just like when you came here that first night when you broke your leg initially. Don't worry! I will make sure you have enough pain medication. I always like to explain to my patients everything they should expect so not to be in shock. I think we will schedule you Monday morning early. Do you have any questions?"

Taking all this new information in all at once at the moment I could not think of any questions I had. I knew internally that I trusted this doctor to repair me back to normal.

Monday came and the surgery was done. I woke up with what I expected, a large cast and pins in my leg. One high close to my thigh and the other two closer to my knee. The pain was as the doctor had mentioned unbearable. Luckily the Dr. was ready with morphine shots in my ass more than once.

I was grateful that this doctor always acted fast I think that is one of the reasons I trusted the man so much. After seeing him twist my leg back around in the emergency room when I first came in weeks ago was very impressive. The best part of all of this was I wasn't tied up like a trussed pig anymore and had a little more movement not much. I was told not to move it or stand on it for two weeks but not having it slung up in the air really was a relief.

Standing up for the first time. I grabbed the crutches and tried to rest them correctly under my armpits and wobbled around. It felt like I was an infant child again trying out my steps learning how to walk for the very first time. Afraid to fall. I did my best to master them I was determined to get better and leave the hospital soon. It reminded me of a new car, just with a flat tire.

Time had passed and I was healing fine. Dr. Halcheck entered my room

"Diego you are doing really well. I am going to release you today but you need to come back in a month so I can take the pins out of your leg and remove the cast. In order to do that I have to put you under again for this and it will only be a same day surgery where you can go home when I am done. If, there are no complications. But I m pretty confident you will be fine. Okay do you have any questions for me?"

I was relieved that I was finally able to leave. I remained to hear what instructions I needed to follow by the nurse that entered. To my surprise she entered with a police officer behind her.

"Are you Diego ?"

"Yes."

"Do you know why I am here?" the officer asked me.

I answered "No why are you hear?" I asked bewildered.

The officer stated "the car you were in on the night of the accident was stolen. And I have orders here from the court to take you to Goshen when you're released here."

"No, I didn't know that the car was stolen that's a surprise to me. I didn't know that guy either. I only met him that night the only thing I know about him is his name and were he works."

"I understand but I still have to follow my orders. I am not going to cuff you I will walk you down to the cruiser." The officer said without any feeling behind his voice one way or the other.

We quietly but very carefully made it out of the hospital me in hospital gown and slippers and my new flat tire. As we approached the door the officer held the door open for me to slide in and he held onto my crutches and placed them in the front seat.

"Now what?" I quietly thought to myself and worried about going to jail for something I did not do and with a leg fresh out of surgery with pins and a cast. How was I going to manage? I tried to keep calm as we arrived at Gosh court house. The officer parked the car and a fancy dressed man approached us.

"Hey leave him I there and come with me to talk to the judge." the fancy dressed man was saying to the officer.

"Don't make him get out he can wait here."

I had no clue to what was going to happen next I could only silently think to myself and try not to worry about what the outcome might be. After what seemed like a short time the police officer and the fancy dressed man approached the car.

"The judge believes that you are a good man. We are not going to send you to jail but release you to your in-laws. I called your wife Linda she says she is with her parents. They have all agreed you can stay there. We will send you a letter when to come back to court at your in-laws house."

The fancy dressed man looked at the police officer and said "drive him there he can show you they way."

CHAPTER 16

Court

Even though Linda and I were living together as husband and wife it was more like two people cohabitating. She did her thing and I did mine. She never made any attempt to be loving or caring in any way. You would think that anyone, even if you did not like them, when they were with someone who was temporarily out of commission. Like in my case fresh out of surgery and still in a cast and with crutches to boot, she would think she would pitch in and do some house work or even cook something for herself. I was getting pretty darn tired of it and was hobbling around on my crutches in the kitchen making myself something simple to eat for lunch. When out of the blue

Whap!

"Oh my God did you just kick me in my leg. What the hell is wrong with you? You and your mother and two sisters are all alike, all four of you belong locked up where no one on the planet has the key."

I was hurting in my leg that had been pinned together from her elephant leg kicking me right were the pins had been put.

"You and your family, except your father, never make any sense at all, always planning and manipulating stuff. Aren't you tired of being such an ass?"

Linda just looked at me with her usual dumb expression on her face like a spoiled little girl and folded her arms across her chest.

"I told you I was hungry and wanted some food too. Why aren't you going to fix me anything I am starving to death?"

"Not by the looks of you no one in there right mind would ever guess that you were starving!"

Later that evening Linda and I were laying down getting ready for the night. I decided I would get up and turn the light off in the hallway so we could get some sleep. As I approached the light switch before my very eyes I saw the switch turn down and the lights went out. Not sure if I imagined it or was seeing things I put the thought behind me and went back to bed. As I laid there in bed I thought about simple matters and I could hear something in the kitchen maybe. I quieted my mind to listen for the sound I thought I heard a moment before, there it goes a gain.

"Brush, BRRUsh, Whish, Whish Scoop."

It sounded like some one was in the kitchen passing a broom across the floor to sweep it. I knew the only people in the small basement apartment was myself and Linda I listened a little harder and there the noise went a again

"Whoosh, Whoosh, Whoosh,"

Wow I knew right then and there that the only answer was that we had a spirit with us. I quietly thought to myself

"One more problem to deal with and this one I could not see."

By this time Linda had wrapped her arms around me in fear because from the looks of things she had heard the same noise I did. I quietly thought that I was more afraid of Linda in this apartment than I was of any spirit. The next morning I got up early to make some coffee and I looked on the counter and looked again. We only had three coffee mugs in the house and one of them had the color of pink lips marked on it.

"What in the world is this "I thought Linda does not wear any lipstick or any makeup for that matter. It was decided that the spirit I heard sweeping the night before was a female ghost what other kind would leave a lipstick print on a coffee mug?

Sometime Linda would spend a few days with her family and I noticed that the apartment would be pretty quiet no noisy ghost sounds but once she would return. The noise and disturbance would start all over again Linda was great at making people hate her, those alive and now one that is a ghost. I use to see spirits all the time when I was younger and I never was fearful.

Knowing that over some parts of my past that a spirit had saved me one way or another I found the female ghost a comfort.

Bright and early one morning Linda, my lawyer and I were all due in court. As we entered we sat down on a long wooden bench that looked like the cleaning crew had polished the varnish almost off of it. I wanted to look around the court to see if I could spot the bastard Miguel who left me there to die in pain and to even perhaps rot in jail for something he did. As I looked around the court house I did not see anyone that looked the even slightest of what I remembered.

Strangely though there was this man on the other side of the court room that kept on staring at my direction with the saddest look on his face.

Every time I would look back at him he would put his head down in such a sad manner I really didn't know what was going on with that man on the other side of the court room.

That man that kept staring at me was a tall very skinny with dark skin and a very large afro style hair.

My fancy lawyer man arrived and sat down next to me but more so in the front to face the Judge. The lawyer I had was my guardian angel. I remembered him saving me before and I was pretty confident he would do a good job for me today.

The judge spoke "Miguel Rodriguez please stand up and address the court. I am ready to read you the charges against you today in this court room."

I noticed the skinny man with the big afro stood up and faced the court. I knew something was wrong but I knew enough to keep quiet until I was able to hear everything and say something later. My heart was beating pretty fast inside my chest I knew all to well how it felt when you are about to face prison or jail when you have done nothing wrong.

The Judge spoke

"Miguel you are being charged with a number of accounts of grand theft auto two to be exact and also reckless driving, leaving a scene of an accident, driving while intoxicated, and driving with out a license. Since these matters are more suited for the grand jury I am going to remand you back to jail until further notice when that can be arranged."

Miguel stayed silent and put his head down, the court room guards cuffed Miguel, the wrong Miguel and escorted him out of the court room and he looked over to me for help. I kept looking at him and he back at me and I could not take it another minute.

"Excuse me your honor I have something very important to say."

The fear in my voice resonated as I spoke.

The judge nodded his head and spoke to me

"Yes Mr. Hillside what is it you would like to say."

"That man you just took out of here is not the man that left me on the side of the road to die. The real Miguel looks much different. My wife was with me at first and she can tell you the same thing." Alright Mr. Hillside said the judge.

"Mrs. Hillside will you please stand up and say your name for the court.

"Yes your honor my name is Linda Hillside."

"Is what Mr. Hillside saying the truth? Was that man not the right person?"

"That is correct your honor that is not the man from Newburgh the man from Newt was 5 foot with light skin and dark short straight hair and brown eyes."

"Okay Mrs. Hillside you may sit down."

"Mr. Hillside what can you tell us about the real Miguel Rodriguez? Do you know where he lives?"

I answered the Judge "No, I don't know where he lives but he mentioned when we were driving around that he worked at a place in Newt called Majestic." The judge then spoke

"We will make an investigation and see if Miguel works there and where Majestic is. Also I need to make a call to get that other man released, he will be going to much better place today then. I really don't want to send the wrong guy to prison."

My lawyer approached the judge and they were talking legal nonsense that I will never understand and returned to where I was sitting and handed me his card.

"We will call you if we need you."

CHAPTER 17

The letter "D"

As always Linda and I were fighting again this morning. About her needs and wants she was always the victim and quite frankly I was sick to death of her crap. Just like any other day earlier this morning another argument ensued over nothing.

"I'm going to my mother's house." Linda said with tears in her eyes from the frustrations of the argument that just past.

"That is the best thing you can do right now." I said

Linda left with a huff and slammed the door behind her.

"Good riddance" I thought

Since it was early and I had some relief with Linda out of the house I got water in a pot to boil for some instant coffee. Waiting for the water to boil I sat down at the kitchen table, I put my head in my hands and started to realize that I needed to make some long over due decisions. I could think clearer with Linda out of the house for a moment as I was reflecting on this. I heard the water for my coffee boiling and I rose to get it and poured myself an instant cup of Maxwell House. As I returned to my chair something caught my attention. Under the table was a square piece of white paper that was not there before. I picked it up. The paper was ice-cold to the touch. On the paper was the capital letter D. It was almost as if some secret force was trying to send me a message. I put the paper down on the kitchen table and thought about different things that would start with the letter D for example names of people and that just did not seem correct. I thought a little longer and it hit me D is the first letter to divorce in English and in Spanish that must be it I thought to myself. At the realization I wondered if it had been the spirit that frequented our apartment from time to time.

73

Thinking, of course, that she had seen the goings on, here with me, and Linda. I suddenly smelled a woman's fragrance like a flowery perfume. The same smell when I thought I felt her presence and at that same moment I felt a wash of coldness go through me.

"I have to make a decision. I think the right decision is to see a lawyer tomorrow"

I remembered I still had the lawyer's card from the car accident and it had his address on it. Luckily for me it was in Little town. On Morgan avenue. Walking distance. It was settled I was going to see the lawyer.

Early the next morning I got dressed and ready for the day ahead, of my beginning to peace of mind. I walked down Academy Avenue and onto Morgan Avenue I found the Lawyers office without any trouble. As I went inside a lovely dressed woman approached with wearing a white business suit, sporting a short hairstyle and sky blue eyes greeted me.

"Hello sir can I help you?" she politely asked me.

"I want to talk to the lawyer, the fancy man his name is on this card."

The woman smiled at me and motioned me to follow her down the hallway to the office.

"What is your name?" She asked

"Diego Diego Hillside." Okay Diego let me get you into see the lawyer. Hello John, this Diego Hillside and he would like to talk to you.

"Take a seat. Would you like some coffee, soda, water?" the lawyer asked as I sat down.

"A regular coffee would be nice."

"Help yourself." He motioned toward the fixings to make myself a cup. After I got my cup of coffee and settled down into the chair he asked me.

"What can I help you with?"

"Well I have had an awful marriage for five year now and I want to know if you can divorce me?" I asked hopefully.

"Mr.Hillside tell me some of the reasons you want a divorce."

"One day my friend Rudy who I have known for years stopped by and wanted me to go with him to Orange to visit some mutual friends we had together. When I started walking down the walk I could here my wife Linda say.

"Keep moving and I will cut my throat. And then I will call the police and tell them that you tried to kill me."

"I of course ignored her and walked towards my friend's car, as I opened the door to the passenger seat I heard her scream. I told my friend that I would have to find out what the hell she was up to and we would get together another time. I went back into my apartment. I could not believe what she did. She had taken one of my straight edge razors and cut her own throat with it and was bleeding now quite a bit.

I did the first thing I could think of and grabbed a towel. I told her if she had gone any deeper she would have actually killed herself and how stupid she was being. Another time I was laying down on the bed just resting and she jumped on the bed with some pillows at first I thought she was just playing around rough housing. Until she put them over my face and held them down to snuff the life out of me. Luckily I was able to get her off of me. I think if I was a weaker man she would have killed me for sure. One other time I had my infant daughter, Elba in my arms who could not have been more than three months at the time. This started a jealous tirade with her mother being jealous that I was holding our daughter who does that? Well one thing led to another and while I had my daughter in my arms she pushed us both into the wall. We could have fallen or worse yet I could have dropped the baby. It did not stop there. I put my daughter in the crib and Linda my wife had gone into the kitchen and grabbed a knife and came at my stomach with it I stopped her with the palm of my hand. Not long after there were sharp knocking on the door it startled me a little but startled me more when I opened it to find two police officers there. Linda still had the knife in her hand.

One of the officers yelled at her to put the knife down and she didn't of course but the one officer managed to take it from her. She is lucky they did not draw their weapons on her. One of the officers told her next time they showed up and if they saw her with a knife they would arrest her. After one of the officers told me I should make a police report. The even asked to make sure I knew where the police office was. Another occasion I was freshly out of the hospital with my leg still in the cast from surgery with pins still holding the bones in place Linda out of the blue just hauled off and kicked me in my broken leg as hard as she could for no apparent reason. We were not arguing or anything that day she just chose to kick me. On many occasions while in bed she would grab hold of my testicles as tight as she could for no reason other than to inflict pain."

At that moment the lawyer put up his hand and said

"That's enough, you know just now you gave me a head ache." The fancy lawyer put his head in his hands and moved his head from side to side rubbing the possible headache I just gave him.

"Let me ask you something? How is it you stayed so long with someone who could have killed you?

The lawyer then also said to me

"do me a favor next time you make the decision to marry, before you say your I do's, take her to the nearest psychiatrist and make very certain she is not crazy like you wife is now. I will talk to the judge this week and I do not see any problem getting you divorced quickly. It will take about ten weeks. You're lucky to be alive; you could have been killed or incarcerated because of her."

I gave the lawyer the address where I was going to be tomorrow morning.

"I'm not going to be living at my address now this is where I am going to be at Pickles farm in Florida New York."

I went back to my apartment and was able to reflect on the decision I had just made feeling the weight lifting off my shoulder. Finally I would have some peace. I heard Linda coming in to the apartment and I jumped up out of bed to talk with her.

"I saw a lawyer today. You have your family and your friends here. I have no one and frankly I do not love you the love I had for you went down the toilet years ago."

No sooner did I say these word Lind true to form started to kick and punch me with all her might. I did what I could to keep her off of me. That night was a long night, I don't think I got any sleep I had one eye open. That was in case Linda decided to something crazy. As soon as daylight came I headed for the taxi stand downtown and got a ride to the Pickles farm in Florida New York.

Exactly ten weeks later I was coming in from the field for lunch and I saw a maroon car parked in front of the small house I lived in now. Inside the car was the lawyer with a folder he handed it to me and said

"These are your divorce papers"

CHAPTER 18

The shortcut

I moved after my divorce to the Falls and found a pretty decent job working in the laundry at Grose Military Academy I really liked the job.

It was out of the elements of the harsh sun, and rain unlike the previous jobs I had working in the various fields. I was visiting a girlfriend of mine, Samantha in Newt it was on my way back to where I knew I could catch the bus back to where I was living.

I decided to walk on Union Avenue to get back unknowing that that road turned out to be a very busy highway with a lot of traffic and fast moving cars.

A few cars had passed by me a little too close. I felt nervous that perhaps one wrong step on the side of the road I would be swiped by a fast moving car. There were no sidewalks where I was walking. About half way down this highway I was relieved to see the laundry building where I worked in the distance and knew I was getting close to where I had to go. Still feeling uneasy about the traffic I climbed over a barbed wire fence to avoid the on coming traffic.

Unfortunately I neglected to see that over the other side of the fence were farm horses, when I got my bearings and stood up. Coming at me was not one big horse but at least a dozen now charging after me.

"What did I do you ask?" I ran as fast as I could to escape the oncoming stampede of horses only to come face to face with another fence that I scaled and brought my self to safety. I was truly scared of the beasts they were all different colors and all very large in size and yes you guessed it fast as shit. As I walked across the yard to the front I could see a little old lady sitting under a big maple tree enjoying the shade from tree. She looked very old and fragile and I really didn't want to scare an innocent old lady sitting there minding her business. I walked over to her and I could see that I was making her nervous. To ease her worries I quickly said.

"Hello miss, I am sorry please don't be nervous I was on the highway walking back to where I worked and was just so worried about getting hit by a car, I climbed over your fence. Are those your big horses?"

"Why yes. Those are my horses, its okay." The old lady now said easing up her worried face.

I put out my hand to introduce myself to her and told her my name and everything else that I worked over at the laundry at Grose Point and lived in the Falls.

"Miss have you lived here long, can I ask you your name?"

The little old lady eased up a little more and told me she had been living there for over thirty five years and her name was Rose. We shared small talk about how nice the country side is and that we both disliked the city type of living. I excused myself and was on my way.

Luckily I managed to catch the bus that would take me back to my house just in time.

About a week later I was working in the laundry when I heard on the loud speaker

"Diego Hillside please come to the office."

Not knowing what that was about, I dropped what I was doing at my job post and went to the office. When I got there I saw my boss talking with someone I did not know sitting in a chair next to him. He was a tall fat man with full facial hair that sported a hefty beard.

As this large man stood up he came over and offered his hand and said

"Hello Diego I am detective Doyle. Can you come with me? I want to ask you some questions about a horse that was killed not too far from here."

The detective turned to my boss and said

"I will bring him back in a little while."

Leaving with the detective we arrived at the local police station and I was escorted into a quite back room. There was another man there as well

"Can I get you some water?"

"Yes please that would be nice."

The detective Doyle focused his eyes on me after the water arrived and started his questioning.

"We understand about a week ago you were at the house where the horse was killed. We got your name and where you worked from the owner when we asked if any strangers had been by and she mentioned you."

"Oh yeah I was there but I only hopped the fence and was very scared of the horses and ran out of there by hopping another fence. I did that because the traffic on the road was so bad. I do not know about killing any horse.!"

"Are you sure you had nothing to do with killing Rose's horse?"

"No I just told you I'm afraid of horses and they were charging after me and I ran away from them I would have to be a giant to kill a horse that size." I now said getting irritated about the fact he wasn't really paying any attention to my story.

"How big was the horse I killed?" I asked purely out of curiosity now.

"Those animals weigh between 1,800 to 2,000 pounds."

"I see and you think a man like me that weighs nothing could be strong enough to kill an animal that size. I would have to be the son of Samson then."

And all of a sudden he said

"We can give you a polygraph and that will tell us if you're lying to us."

"Sure I can take that test. I am not lying to you."

No sooner had the detective mentioned the polygraph, he changed his questioning to something even more ridiculous.

"Well were you trying to steal one of those horses then?"

"What? What would I do with a horse? I don't like horses I have tried to tell you now all afternoon I am afraid of horses?"

"They won't hurt you they are just docile farm animals."

I was starting to get tired about us getting no where with the questioning going around in circles. I don't know why but I decided to say I did it.

"You know what I killed the horse with a stick I had."

"Where did you put the stick then?

Really? I thought to myself this guy is a real dick, so I decided to play along since he was obviously being ridicules. I decided to have some fun.

"I think I threw it out onto the road where I was walking."

"Okay then you're under arrest and I want you to show us where the stick is. Put your hand out in front of you."

The detective Doyle another officer and I got into the squad car and went to where I had thrown the invisible stick that I like Samson had killed this giant horse. I noticed cars were slowing down and people were looking at us me in my new bracelets and the officers combing the area. They finally gave up and drove me to the court house. Since I was charged with a misdemeanor of hitting a horse I never met with the invisible stick I found myself face to face with a Judge who remanded me into custody until my court hearing.

This is because it you do not have money to post bail you sit and wait for your time to speak in court to defend yourself. Around ten days later I faced the judge with my public defender who was pissed at me because I had confessed to something I did not do and was pleading my case in court as best he could

"Your honor how do you suppose a man of approximately 190 pounds would have the strength to kill an animal of that size and weight? And with one stick? It seems to me that the only way that could be possible is if Mr. Hillside had a gun with him that day and shot the horse in the head or if he owned the horse and starved him to death. I don't know of another way this could be. Look at him your honor he is just a scrawny guy compared to the majestic size of those farm animals that is used. I ask that you take this into consideration before you give Mr. Hillside any time at all for the misdemeanor of hitting a horse with a branch which by the way was never found."

"The problem Mr. Hillside we have your confession that you said yourself you hit the horse so I have to in my own conscience whether it happened or not and follow the law and sentence you. Even if perhaps you did not do the thing you said you did. The law predicts that when a crime is confessed that there has to be some sort of punishment or restitution. Perhaps in the future if you are innocent of any crime you will use your right to request a lawyer. For that matter I am sentencing you to 60 days in the county jail followed by five years of probation." The judge said finally and slammed the gavel on his podium.

I was driven back to OCJ or as other may recall it by its full name Orange County Jail in Gosh New York this is where all persons go that have less than a year sentence. I managed to maintain a reasonable amount of decorum with the others in there doing their time and One day Nelson another inmate who was doing time for something stupid asked me

"Hey man, what did you do to get locked up in this asshole of a place?" He nodded my way.

"Well if you can believe it I am in here for killing a horse with my bare hands or a stick they say."

"What the hell? What size horse was it?"

"According to the county the horse I killed by myself was between 1,800 to 2,000 lbs." I said sort of chuckling to myself even saying it out load sounded so absurd.

"WHAT!!!? You're kidding right? You would have to be the strongest man in the world. Is your middle name Samson?" Nelson now asked smiling to me wide eyed at the prospect that perhaps I was a strong as Samson.

I was muscular from all the hard labor but really not strong enough to kill a horse. As soon as this info was out it spread like wild fire through the jail and the officers of the jail and inmates a like all called me

Son of Samson. My 60 days came fast enough and I learned to stand my ground next time I am accused of anything I did not do.

CHAPTER 19

Walking on the road again

I had just been released from Orange County Jail and walking straight to Little town New York this time, there were no shortcuts to get me into trouble. Five miles straight up the road in one direction thank God.

I ended up on the longest street of little town New York called North street. While on the sidewalk I heard a woman's voice not sure where it was coming from or even if the voice was meant for me. I heard it again

"Come here you down there."

I stopped walking and looked around to find this strange voice and looked up to see a woman's head peeking out of the third story window of an apartment building above where I had been standing.

I answered

"Are you talking to me?"

The head in the window asked "do you live here? In Little town I mean?"

What a strange way to meet someone I thought to myself I answered back

"I lived here a few years ago"

The head now said to me in return

"I never saw you here before. what is your name?"

I obliged with an answer

"Diego."

The woman's head now answered

"My name is Carol"

Now the strange woman's head in the window had a name to it Carol. We continued talking me on the sidewalk and her with her head out the window. While we were talking, the slight, aroma of, coffee being brewed.

I said "I smell coffee."

"Oh that's me I am making coffee that is what you must smell. Do you like coffee?" the woman now with a name asked me.

"Um yes." I answered

"Wait one minute I will be right down," Carol said.

After a few minutes the woman's head from the window appeared at the front door with a body attached to it.

I asked "where is the coffee?"

Carol motioned for me to enter the building and to follow her up a long flight of stairs. I noticed that almost each and every step I landed on squealed as if it was being hurt. Carol lived all the way on the third floor we entered into her apartment and she invited me to sit down. When Carol returned with the hot coffee in hand she asked me

"Where do you live?"

I answered "I have just been released from Orange County Jail so right now I am looking for perhaps a room in one of the rooming houses here." I said answering her question.

"Why were you in jail? That is if you don't mind me asking?"

I answered her question

"Believe it or not I was in there for sixty days for killing an 18hundred pound horse."

Laughing now slightly Carol looked at me a little bewildered and said

"You're kidding right?"

"No I am telling you the truth I was in there for sixty days like I said. I was innocent but had to do that time because for whatever reason they thought it was possible."

Now blinking her eyes quite rapidly Carol looked at me and exclaimed

"That was ridiculous what they did to you are they morons there in the town of Goshen? No one can kill a horse that way, only perhaps if they take a gun and shoot the horse. A horse can kill a man not the other way around." Carol now said exasperated.

We both continued to drink our coffees and enjoyed the rest of the afternoon talking about minor things about the town and what was going on in here life. Not too long after this nice quiet conversation with the nicely brewed coffee I found myself living in that third floor apartment with Carol. It did not take long and I was introduced to her daughter

Marisol and her four grandchildren, two girls and two boys the girls were almost teenagers and the boys younger around the same age boys are when there in grammar school.

One afternoon Carol and her daughter invited me to accompany them on a trip to New York City it was about an hour and a half drive and the ladies wanted to do some shopping in the city I decided to go but later regretted it. The trip consisted of me and the children stuck in the car while Carol and Marisol would go into the shops to look and always it seems came out with nothing in their hands this seemed to go for ever.

We finally returned home in the morning hours. I thought to myself secretly

"Next time I will not go with these ladies who could find it exciting to shop the night away and return home with nothing to show for it."

A few weeks had gone by and Marisol was asking me

"Diego I know you did not enjoy yourself last time mom and I went to the city to shop, and you and the kids get along so well. Would you mind very much watching them here at my apartment while mom and I go into the city tonight?" She asked with a look of expectation in her eyes.

"That is fine. I can stay here and watch the kids for you. I would rather do that then sit in the car all night."

Carol and Marisol left in the van and trusted me to remain watching the four kids. I thought what I could do to entertain them so to keep them happy and out of trouble. I decided to take an old towel and cut two eye holes out of them and put the towel over my head completely and taped it around my neck to not fall off.

I was trying to replicate the Monster from the Frankenstein movies I had remembered seeing as a boy.

I did this and walked dragging one foot behind me and moaning like the monster did in the movie chasing the kids. They either hid in the closet or under the bed or behind the couch, When I was close enough I grabbed and tickled them and they laughed and screamed quite loud. I tired of being the monster and resorted to being Dracula and put strawberry jam in the corners of my mouth for some true effect and grimaced my face to resemble Dracula as best as I could and commenced chasing all the children again, we did this for some time and I noticed I tired all of them out. Funny it was almost immediately I saw them go to their rooms and they were fast asleep. I thought to myself

"I must have tired them out pretty good."

I actually had a lot of fun that night as well and settled down on the recliner with now what was a nice cup of tea I had just made for myself and turned on the television to wait for the ladies to return.

Some time later that year in early winter as I was sitting by myself drinking a cup of tea I heard a quickened footstep coming up the stairs.

"KNOCK, KNOCK"

I opened up the door, Marisol there at the doorway out of breath. She caught her breath as best as anyone could after climbing the steps to the third floor.

"Diego do you think you can watch my apartment while mommy and I go to New York?" She asked me between her huffs and puffs of catching her breath.

"Okay." I answered and put on my shirt and shoes

found a light jacket even though winter was not here yet it was starting to get colder lately.

I followed Marisol down the three flights of stairs to where the van was waiting for her and me at the street level. I did not think too much of it but I noticed all the grandkids were there in the van too, looking sharp for a trip to the city. At the time I did not think much of the fact they were all going except me. Not that I minded not going but I found something was not right I just could not put my finger on it. I arrived at Marisol's apartment a few minutes later went to the kitchen made myself a cup of tea and decided to snap the TV on. As I sat down and had a moment to myself I wondered silently why it was necessary for me to be there. I mean they all went and she really had nothing of importance or value in her apartment. It locked like all other apartments in Little town. I thought to myself after a while I do not need to remain here, nothing is going to happen. I put my cup in the sink and made sure the stove was off grabbed my light jacket, turned off the TV set and headed for the door. When I reached the front door the TV turned itself on and as I stood in front of the opened front door I felt a strange invisible energy holding me back.

In a flash there was a light a white light the shape of an orb circling now and heading down the hallway to the first bedroom.

"Weird." I thought to myself quietly.

Something or some force for whatever reason was telling me not to leave. What in the world can be going on here I wondered silently. I took my jacket back off and sat back down in the chair I was just sitting in. I could see down the hallway to the apartment and a flash of light again. I could see this from the corner of my eyes sitting there frozen in my chair I watched this orb of light dance around in circles and enter into the same bedroom again.

"What on earth can this mean?" I wondered silently a little nervous but knew somehow this flash of light was trying it's hardest to tell me something but what? I went to the kitchen and fixed myself a cup of green tea with honey and returned to the chair in the living room as I sipped my tea, There it was again circling the same areas in the hallway and again went straight into the same bedroom.

"What on earth?" I asked myself silently now a little still in the chair.

Out of the blue I heard the sound of a young baby crying. I did not think too much of it since this apartment building had other families with small children and thought perhaps the babies cry belonged to a child in one of the neighbor's apartment. The babies cries got louder and I instantly thought of my daughter long ago and wondered just for a moment was it my past coming back to haunt me? I put my hand up to my forehead in dismay not understanding why was I hearing now a very loud cry of a small baby? Was I going crazy? No, I was a sane as anyone else. I thought again, I here it again that is a real live baby crying and it is close too close to be the neighbor's baby. The crying got louder and louder then the ball of light got brighter and bigger and circled around and went straight into the same bedroom it had gone into earlier. I stood up carefully and crept into the bedroom slowly not sure what I was about to find in there. I looked at the bed and to my utter dismay I saw something moving under a very large comforter. I froze for a moment back in time to when I had found Elba in the same circumstance. I shook myself out of that and uncovered the crying infant and picked the baby up. The child was out of breath from crying hysterically under the blanket that was smothering it I was so upset and afraid.

Number one this child almost died and I had no idea the child was here and second whose baby is this. I walked carefully, now embracing the infant to the living room where there was light and could tell by the clothing he had on that this was a baby boy. He looked to be maybe four or five months of age with beautiful hazel eyes and blonde hair. From the looks of him he appeared to be a healthy young baby. His coloring had finally returned and the crying had stopped to a light whimper when someone had been crying for a while. I thought to myself that he must be hungry since I really had no idea how long he had been here. I fixed the child a warn bottle of formula while I held him in my arms, not wanting this young child upset again. Sitting down with him he drank the bottle of milk I had prepared. I held him with love for a baby a stranger could give and him to know he was safe now that I knew he was here. Secretly though I thought about Carol and Marisol and how evil the two of them really were. I knew I would get the bottom of this or at lease sort out my own feelings after this night pass.

The small baby fell asleep on the sofa nearby where I was sitting. I covered him this time with a lighter blanket to not let him be smothered. I watched his angelic face as he slept and had the look of peacefulness on his face. I thought about the white orb that was here earlier was it a guardian angel for the baby or for both of us? I could not stop thinking about what could have happened to both of us if this had ended up with a dead infant and me here to take the blame of some evil set up by the people that said they cared about me. I reflected that I almost left this apartment to leave behind an innocent child and myself an innocent man who would have paid the ultimate price of freedom Oh my God thank you for stopping me I kept saying to myself. Marisol, Carol and the kids returned from the city returned home and never said a word to me like is the baby okay or did you have any trouble with the baby.

I stayed there in the chair thinking quietly to myself. There was a knock at the door. I got up to answer it since everyone had run to the beds to sleep. I saw a beautiful young girl on the other side of the door I asked her

"Are you looking for someone?" She nodded her head and said

"I am looking for my son Johnny."

"Oh that's your baby?" I asked her taking a mental note of what she looked like. The young pretty girl nodded.

I knew that someday in the near future I would find this young mother and tell her everything that happened here tonight just not now. I wanted to see what these two crazy bitches would say, if anything, about this young child in the next few days.

Not too long after as I was walking on the street to get some fresh air I saw the young woman and the small baby walking in my direction.

"Hello, do you remember me from the other morning?" I asked hoping she did.

"Yes I remember you opened the door when I went to pick up Johnny."

"Yes that's right I need to talk to you but I need you to promise me something, to keep this a secret between us and I want you looking at me right into my eyes."

The young woman moved as close to me as possible.

"Those two women you trusted your baby with left the city and left your little son behind under a large quilt like blanket. They never said to me one word that he was even there. Thank God I heard your baby crying I found him struggling under that blanket trying to breathe and crying. Your son would have died if I never saw him there and I would have gone to prison an innocent man due to the actions of Carol and Marisol."

The young woman started to cry holding her baby closer to her now.

"Oh my, God. God bless for being there and saving my baby." she held me tight now as well.

"Do me a favor never trust those two women ever not for anything. I was so mad I could not think straight for days I am leaving because this was unforgivable. I have a place to go never trust them again. Okay?"

She nodded and hugged me and walked away.

The world has been lifted off my shoulders now that I had the chance to tell that young woman what happened. I knew she would never trust her child with them ever again. I thought to myself

"I am going to visit my new girlfriend Toby."

CHAPTER 20

A New Path

July 16, 1998 *started a new day living with my girlfriend of long ago.*
We had known each other in the past and perhaps if things had worked out
better for us in the past

We would perhaps already have had a life behind us with memories
you get when you're married. Not everything in life works out that way
though. Sometimes life takes longer to get you onto the path you should
have taken or stayed on in the first place.

Toby and her two children lived on a very quiet street that everyone
referred to as little Italy. I think because there was an Italian bakery
down one street Italian restaurant on another street and a Italian grocery
convenience store on another street everything in walking distance. The
neighbor's for the most part were Italian, also there was this little four
foot high Italian lady Marie that stood out the most to me. She had
the garden of all gardens, grapes, tomatoes, apricots, broccoli wonderful
and always happy when Maria was not attending her garden for some
reason she would sweep her pristine driveway. My girlfriend and I would
spend lots of hours on her front porch talking, playing cards or just
sipping wine. Her house was a two story yellow butter cream siding very
attractive looking on the side of the porch were clinging roses that were
the envy of everyone that just happened to walk by. "I felt joy here a
peace I had never had for myself in all my life a quiet little street with
nice surroundings. My girl Toby worked at the hospital up the hill and
I would walk her to work every morning to keep her company. I liked
doing this it helped me to start my own day.

While I was getting use to this better way of life and her children
were getting use to me I decided to make a go at doing my own garden

in the back yard it was big enough and I knew in my heart that everyone would benefit from it. I planted tomatoes, corn, and broccoli.

The back yard was fenced in and I felt at times that I was in my own little sanctuary a life that was long over do. I was happy. I met Toby's father Joe who I liked right away. He was short and stocky and had a very nice personality he made it a point to stop by once every so often to see his grandchildren Annete and Peter would at times take us out to lunch. One particular morning Joe was looking at my garden and

"Boy Diego you could be a farmer. Just look at the size of those tomatoes."

I shook my head in agreement.

"What time is Tobye off from work?" He asked using the nickname he had for my girlfriend.

I answered "she is done around three today."

Joe looked up to the sky as if he was thinking something quietly to himself and said

"Hey you want to go to Home Depot and look around?"

"Sure why not. Let me just make sure the doors are locked."

We took a short ride to the local Home Depot and managed to end up in the nursery section I noticed Joe eyeing a young tree.

"What do you think Diego, this is a plum tree do you think it would look nice in the back yard?"

"Sure I don't see why not. I know how to plant it fine and it should bring lots of fruit later."

"Okay let's get it and we can plant it together this will be our tree. What do you say?"

Joe was so excited about finding the plum tree in the first place and for me to do something together with him felt very good to me that day. The plum tree was planted and after some months it had thousand of white blossoms on it we all marvel in its beauty and each took turns taking pictures under it. The tree ripened and produced some of the pretties purplish blue plum fruits I had ever seen. It produced so many that we of course, shared some with other family members and of course with Joe.

One morning as I was walking around town I spotted a red men's bicycle outside in a neighbors driveway with a for sale sign on it. Five dollars.

"It can't be right I thought to myself. Better go and see if there is anything wrong with it and I think if there is no problem. I have five bucks in my pocket."

I proceeded up the neighbor's driveway.

"Are you selling that bike for five dollars?" I asked hoping that is was not a mistake.

"Yes. Why, do you want it?" The old lady asked raising her garden hat up to see me better with the sun beaming in here eyes.

"Yes."

"You can have it. Five bucks and you can take it. The bike will be all yours."

I looked at it and it appeared to be fine I chose not to ask questions and handed the elderly lady my five dollars.

I had not been on a bicycle since my childhood. When I use to rent a bike ride for five cents a half hour from Lou. He was the only one in my neighborhood that could actually afford one. Butt I guess five cents was Pretty cheap. I rode that bicycle I bought from the old Woman almost everyday. It gave me the freedom to see things you would not normally see in a car.

My girlfriend's house was not too far from the church Where my daughter Elba was buried and I would ride up to the church on Cottage Street. It was one of the bigger Catholic churches in the area. Toby and I often would attend since it was a nice walk from the house. My days were peaceful spent riding the bike or picking up my girlfriend from her job. Or simply making dinner for the family. I would make homemade fried chicken and French fried potatoes. The kids loved that.

Some time had passed, we all got to be comfortable.

"Diego I think now that we are getting pretty good at managing our money and stuff. I think it is time we both get our license. I need to retake all of my testing and I know you never had a license what better way to do a project together, that will benefit both of us.

What do you think?" Tobye asked me as she sipped the wine I had just poured for her outside on the front porch.

I looked at her and thought about it before I answered her. Secretly I was a little afraid that it would not work out. If you looked at the hardships I endured in the past. I replied.

"I think we can. What do we have to do?"

"We need to get our permits first by passing a written test. They have a new law now that we need to take a safety class first in order to get our permits. I am sure it is mostly watching films and learning how dangerous it is to drink and drive."

I knew that all to well considering the three scars left on my leg from getting a fractured femur because of some asshole driving drunk. We both endured the boring but necessary classes until the end. Both of us took driving lessons. Funny our road test was scheduled on the same day. We both received our licenses the next week.

I was feeling great and seeing that my life was progressing for the better every day.

Our first car together, if you can call it that was a blue Monte Carlo that shook like a wet dog when you started it up and smoked like a dragon in the back. We chose not to go far in it. We had bought the car from the Liar down the street for three hundred dollars and later sold

It back to him for five hundred what a dummy. I should have nicknamed him dummy but liar was what had stuck. He was called that because he went around telling everyone that he owned a hundred acres of land somewhere. More like that hundred acre wood that Winnie the Poo has in make believe land.

Time had passed and we had a decent savings between us. I managed to buy myself a used green Ford Ranger truck with a canopy. Nothing fancy just something to help me get around to get gardening supplies and once in a while I would take a drive to Orange Island to see old friends of mine. Men who I had worked with out in the onion fields years ago. It felt like a lifetime ago. Toby and the kids had a better car to get around in too, one that doesn't shake or smoke.

Some months later I was in the cemetery talking to my daughter, enjoying being outdoors. The cemetery was well maintained and cared for. This particular morning I had chose to ride my bicycle there. I headed home and drove the bike into the driveway. Something looked strange and different.

"Holy shit! My truck! It was here when I left I have the key in my pocket. Where did it go?"

Putting the bike into the garage I walked up the driveway to the front door and went inside.

"Hey my truck is gone. Did you see anyone here taking it?" I asked exasperated.

Toby came closer to me and said

"Your truck is on its way to Florida. After you left a little while later a man who drives cars on his hauler truck to other states for a living drove your truck away To Florida" looking at me to make sure I understood.

"What did you do that for?" I asked upset.

"I wanted to make sure you came with me to Florida and start our lives together."

I wasn't sure to be mad or happy at the moment. I at least knew where my truck was going. We were moving to Florida and after all I guess the idea of driving from NY to Florida twice just seemed like too much.

CHAPTER 21

My Return Home

Some time had passed and we were settled in our new home in Florida.

"You know Diego you have not been to your home in over thirty three years. Don't you miss some of your family? You know some of them are elderly now like your aunts and uncles. We have a little money left from the sale of the house. Why don't we go to a travel agent tomorrow and get what we need for airfare and hotel. This way when we are tired of visiting and sight seeing we can go back to our hotel room and relax." Toby said this with real concern for me not seeing my family for so many years.

September 15th the limo for the airport was honking its horn outside. I was still dead tired I think I only had about thirty minutes of sleep.

Getting on the plane heading back to Puerto Rico brought back so many feelings and memories. The childhood games I had played with my brother. The beatings and hardships provided by my father. The goodbyes I made with my loving grandparents now dead. Knowing that I never made it back to visit them still bothered me.

"Wake up were here already."

It felt like a dream as if I was still in a dream world. I had so many emotions it was hard to get a handle on which emotion to go with. Sadness, anger, excitement, or resolve. I decided to enjoy myself for Toby's sake. We headed for Cellomar hotel and casino what a beautiful place. Surrounded by water, and country side. In our hotel we had a beautiful view of the ocean and pools down below off of our balcony.

"Oh my God, Puerto Rico is so beautiful I can't believe you ever left here." Toby said.

Since I needed time to prepare myself for the family visits I thought maybe a little pumping and sweating in the bed would be a good idea. We chose to leave the door open with the sounds of the waves crashing to muffle our sounds of ecstasy. Later that evening I called my sister Evelyn to let her know we were in Puerto Rico and what hotel we were in. We made arrangements for her to come and pick us up the next morning.

Evy made it to our hotel pretty early as we drove back to my hometown I noticed so many new houses and changes that had taken place over the years.

Our first stop was my grandparent's houses were I remembered the love my grandpa had for me and the jokes about the money tree. Grandmas cooking so many thoughts came flooding back to the time when I was a young boy. Happy here with them.

Wishing I could hold them once more to let them know that I was fine. My sister parked her car and we all got out.

In the center of the yard was a big Tamarind fruit tree that is indigenous to Puerto Rico. Under the shade tree were two of my uncles Angel and Nando. They were my grandmother's sons. I noticed some other older men sitting around the tree and one resting in a hammock another sitting at the root of the tree.

"Hey tanto tiemo what happened to you? Did you forget everybody?" My one uncle said as showed the shock of seeing me standing in front of him.

I went over to both my uncles and gave them both a healthy squeeze. After some introductions my two nephews whom I have never met came walking up and asked right away.

"Uncle Diego do you want some coconut water?"

My nephews Ali and Nester were two nice looking young teenagers with wonderful manners. Out in the distance I could see a tall figure walking up to the tree on hand held a cigar the other a Budweiser beer. Here was the Octopus aged and dirty looking surprised that I was standing there under the tree talking with my nephews.

"When did you get here?" was the only thing my father thought to say.

I think he was in shock to see me standing there. As I looked his way feeling nothing. I did not care if he was alive or dead just another old dirty man that had a habit of drinking and smoking. I thought to myself.

"The past is the past. I will never forget what you did."

Keeping these thoughts inside actually hurt, we all left. Later we went to the house were I grew up.

My mother and fathers house we walked through the front door and quickly out the back, that was all I needed no feeling of warm fuzzy goodness just darkness. Leaving there was the best thing I ever did for myself.

Cursing the past, quietly to myself. We made it to the cemetery where my grandparents were laid to rest in a mausoleum. I thought it was good now that they had more security at the graveyard. As you entered you had to sign a paper to say why you were there and who's grave or burial site you were visiting.

We returned to the Tamarind tree. I gave all the elderly men some money I left behind over eight hundred dollars that day. We stopped to visit my two aunts and spent some time there. My cousin was there also.

I asked my uncles about my friends I grew up with and sadly most if not all had died of drugs or alcohol.

I would have loved to have seen them. The afternoon was coming quickly Evelyn drove us to a little restaurant that served mostly fish this was wonderful fresh fish actually caught that day. Toby decided this was her favorite place to eat. Ordered more fish to take home later and also frozen fish to bring on the plane. They had Marlin, red snapper, fresh lobster any kind of fish you could think of. After lunch we headed back to visit the street I had to walk back and forth to school. I remembered this was the very first place I ever saw a spirit in my life. I can still see the little boy running in the park and when I ran to catch up to him he had vanished.

We made it back to the big tree to let everyone know we were heading back to the hotel but would make sure we stopped back again before we had to leave. Later that night feeling a little bored Toby and I decided to visit the casino that was right across the courtyard from our hotel. Toby was winning and I saw some women telling her to stop. She eventually did.

"Hey I won over four hundred dollars I think I want to get my self some local pina coladas. Now that I have a little extra money I can afford to drink a couple."

Feeling that I wanted to try my luck a little more I said "okay, I am going to try my luck a little more. I will meet you in the bar in a little while."

I went to a slot machine I thought would give me luck nope, nothing. Remembering the ATM machine outside the casino I headed there. From nowhere behind me I felt a tap tap tap on my shoulder.

"What the hell are you doing?"

I turned to see my girlfriend there. Not feeling I need to explain to her I said. "I need some more money so I am going to take it."

"Oh no you're not what happens if you spend all of the money and we end up sitting here like two big dummies give me that card I will give you some cash I have here in my pocket."

I was a little pissed but agreed and held up the card she grabbed it and handy me a twenty!!!

"What am I suppose to do with that?"

"What ever you want I will be at the bar!"

After I cooled down I realized she saved me from spending the rest of our money. I think I was about to take out two hundred out glad I didn't.

I called my sister and made more plans for the rest of the week. Time flew by. We had my sister and her two boys over one night while they swam in the pool my sister and I enjoyed talking on the balcony.

The morning came for us to leave. It had turned out to be a good trip seeing all of my family and where I grew up. I was ready to go back to our new home in Florida.

The limo came for us and we arrived with extra time to spare both feeling hungry we stopped at a hotdog vender seeing there was nothing else we paid five bucks a hotdog. Can you believe it? Highway robbery.

I guess both of us forgot to check the weather and did not realize we were in hurricane Bill until we were up in the air in the airplane. When I left Puerto Rico it was in a thick fog now a hurricane.

Notes from Toby

Well we made it home…….. I chose to write this story for Diego. It pained me to see all of the suffering he had endured over the years. Diego never told me anything about his childhood until that day when the tears started flowing that day on the front porch. I wrote this

As he spoke it. It had to be courageous to face these old shadows of yesteryear ……….

We have been together seventeen years this July. I love him with all my heart.

Toby

The End